Good to Grow

Reorienting Your Business for Unstoppable Growth

I0149651

Todd Garretson

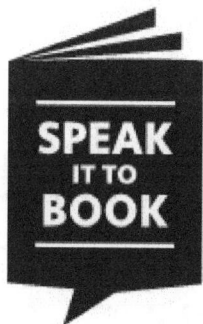

SPEAK
IT TO
BOOK

Speak It To Book
www.speakittobook.com

Good to Grow / Todd Garretson
ISBN-13: 978-1945793189
ISBN-10: 194579318X

*To Mom and Dad, thank you for instilling in me the enduring values of hard work, honesty, and commitment. I **grew** because of you.*

*To Lauri, my dearest wife and best friend, your endless faith, encouragement, and confidence in me is everything. I've **grown** because of you.*

*And for Lauren, Landon, Lex, and Lily ... my prayer is that you uncover God's amazing plan for your life. Get ready to **grow** beyond what you think is possible.*

CONTENTS

A Note from the Author

Thank you for investing in *Good to Grow: Reorienting Your Organization for Unstoppable Growth*!

From a very young age, I remember my mom and dad dragging my little brother and me to our family manufacturing business on Saturdays while they both tended to business that needed handling. My brother and I learned the family business from the ground up. From the time I could walk, I remember helping my mom and dad sweep floors, stock shelves, and pack and ship products to customers. I (not so fondly) remember packing boxes in the factory during the hot Pennsylvania summers with no air conditioning. I was raised to value commitment, hard work, and honesty.

Many hot summers, diplomas, and degrees later, my brother and I finally (somehow) graduated out of the factory and into the air-conditioned office area, where we were awarded desks in a cubicle and were tasked to sift through miles of "green bar" sales reports while we pounded out data, charts, and graphs. This was *way* before salesforce.com, fancy MacBooks, and smartphones. Officially joining my father's family business full-time, I completely entrenched myself in what became a 24-hour-a-day, 365-day-a-year "mission to the top."

With an intense desire to be productive and make an impact, I laddered through a number of sales and marketing leadership roles within the family business and later climbed many rungs on the Fortune 500 ladder.

In my climb to the top, I finally found the step on the ladder that suited me. I discovered my true passion—and where I excelled most—was in the one-on-one time I spent with employees and customers, educating, coaching, consulting, and advising them on strategies to improve and grow. Those kinds of interactions just seemed to work—and produced results. On that rung of the ladder, I could immediately see the wider circle of potential around customers' businesses and relished crafting the plan to help them realize their potential.

And that's why I decided to embark on writing this book. The chase for *potential*.

My desire is that your next big growth idea or break-through strategy might be inspired by something you read on the pages that follow.

I've structured this book in a way to allow for maximum growth for the reader. Thus, accompanying each chapter of the book is a set of reflective questions, with an application-oriented summary provided as an "action step." These workbook sections are included as a tool to help you and your leadership team understand what it takes to foster a consistent, growth-oriented, people-first business culture that can flourish during these rapidly changing times—when decades-old conventional wisdom about effective strategy and leadership has been tossed out the window.

By the time you finish this book and have responded to the questions in the workbook and throughout the manuscript, you'll have a strategic vision, as well as practical ideas for reorienting your business toward a bright future of sustainable growth.

So, are you ready to delve into some of your most important growth challenges? Growth-centered organizations do much more than grow numbers; they grow people, customers, and value. If you're ready for consistent, sustainable growth, then join me—and get ready to *GROW* for it!

—Todd Garretson

INTRODUCTION

Ready, Set, Grow!

Do you feel like you are barely surviving as a business leader? Do you desire to drive growth for tomorrow but feel like you have hit a plateau? Are you beginning to doubt your strategy? Are you desperate to unlock dormant growth potential in your organization—and in your personal life?

The book you hold in your hand is more than a book on growth. It is an *opportunity*. Consider it a personal challenge to step out of line and take a stand, to build and lead a strong, growth-centered organization. According to businesswoman Cynthia Occelli, who has written and spoken extensively on personal empowerment and growth, "For a seed to achieve its greatest expression, it first must come completely undone. The shell cracks, its insides come out and everything changes. To someone who doesn't understand growth, it would look like complete destruction."[1]

In the same way, personal growth—which directly impacts how you lead and, thus, your organization's growth—can often feel like "complete destruction." Building a growth-organization is not easy. Sometimes you might need to become "completely undone" before growth can happen.

However, if you are ready to commit to reading the pages that follow, consider some of the tips and tools offered, embrace personal transformation, and the call to build people first, you just might be ready for growth beyond what you ever imagined.

CHAPTER ONE

Grow Out of Your Way:
Creating a Growth-Oriented Culture

Why don't we grow?

It's a question that all of us, as business leaders, ask ourselves at one time or another—and usually more often than we'd like. We hypothesize as to why the strategy didn't work. We theorize on why earnings didn't increase. And we argue over the reasons sales didn't climb.

But rarely do we spend any time asking, "Why didn't he or she grow?"

Prominent business news publications have run feature articles on the daunting challenge leaders face in balancing the demands of their personal and professional lives. A Fast Company article entitled "What Are Americans Most Stressed Out About" cited everything from "juggling too many responsibilities" to "relationships" to "finances" as some of the major stressors people face head-on daily.[2]

Moreover, studies show that the way people cope with these stressors is ultimately by sleeping less, eating less, and exercising less. Follow the dominoes a little further down the path and you're likely to find yourself with major health issues, lack of energy, and depression. In a *Harvard Business Review* article entitled "Making Business Personal," the authors shared their search for the deliberately developmental organization—which essentially is an "organization that is committed to developing every one of their people by weaving personal growth into daily work." After searching the globe, they found only twenty such companies. Ultimately, one conclusion was that "professional and personal growth in organizations is interdependent."[3]

Two Strategic Challenges

Columbia business professor and author Rita McGrath has outlined the top strategic challenges for companies.[4] Here are the top two challenges she identified:

1. Companies are not confident in their talent. In research studies, many top executives cite they simply "don't have the right or enough leaders to lead the growth projects."
2. Companies are worried about growth. In particular, with respect to innovation, organizations don't have the right processes in place to deliver a repeatable and steady stream of new products or services to the marketplace.

These top two challenges McGrath described thus center squarely on growth as a priority, straight from the C-suite. There is no bigger challenge or need organizations have right now than how to create and deliver repeatable growth.

If you are a manufacturing business or retailer in the mid-market space, the above issues are even more relevant and timely. Chances are, if you're like most, you're buried in today's weeds, without the strategy or in-house talent to drive the innovation you need to deliver growth in the short- and long-term. If you fail to jump on the right path now, you will risk losing market share to up-and-coming, nimbler, and more technologically advanced organizations.

The Bold Road to Growth

If we take a step back for a moment, it is fascinating to consider the end-to-end journey a person or business endures to move from a current state to an enhanced state of being—also referred to as 'change.' Or better yet, 'growth.'

The sequence of events leading to change might look something like the following "path to change" sequence:

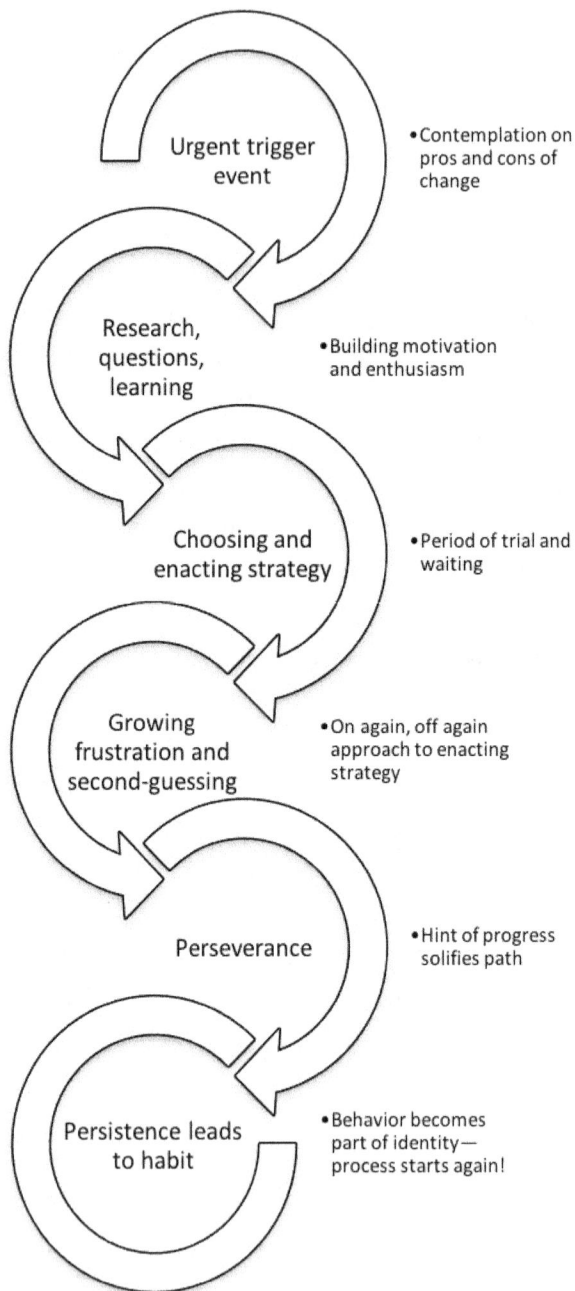

Urgent trigger event

• Contemplation on pros and cons of change

Research, questions, learning

• Building motivation and enthusiasm

Choosing and enacting strategy

• Period of trial and waiting

Growing frustration and second-guessing

• On again, off again approach to enacting strategy

Perseverance

• Hint of progress solifies path

Persistence leads to habit

• Behavior becomes part of identity— process starts again!

Only a small percentage of businesses and individuals endure the messy middle sections of this cyclical process. Make no mistakes about it: the periods of trial,

> **While accountability is easy to skirt, honesty is not.**

waiting, growth, and frustration will make you think it's risky to keep going and that there is nothing worthwhile on the other side. However, those who succeed learn to accept, and even embrace, the wrestling, scratching, and clawing that happen in the middle of pursuing growth.

So, why are some people (very few) comfortable with being uncomfortable? Perhaps they're unsettled with the alternative—staying the same.

Are you bold enough to grow?

Let's Be Honest About Growth

When it comes to growth, however, boldness is not enough. In fact, there could not be a more perfect starting point for growth than honesty.

And honesty isn't simply a matter of not lying. It's much more. 'Honesty' is a better word for 'accountability.' Yes, it's a word that sounds old-fashioned, but I vote to bring honesty back in a big way. While accountability is easy to

> **Honesty is who you are and how you live your life. Honesty is not only telling the truth; it's also seeking the truth.**

skirt, honesty is not. When accountability is only a buzzword tossed carelessly about in corporate management meetings, it's honesty that stands solid as a rock.

Honesty is *who you are* and *how you live your life*. Honesty is not only telling the truth; it's also *seeking* the truth. In the Bible, the apostle John put it this way:

> *Then you will know the truth, and the truth will set you free.* — *John 8:32 (NIV)*

There is nothing that will hamper your growth pursuit more than a lack of truth or a general resistance to seek the truth. Equally, there is nothing more freeing and liberating than a clean slate. Imagine how much further and faster you could go if you didn't have a trailer of heavy baggage to pull.

Thus, the story of honesty:

Honesty is not afraid to ask the hard questions. Honesty digs for the truth, accepts the truth, and lives by the truth no matter what. Whether it's faith, family or business, honesty seeks to understand first.

> *You can find honesty in the back of the room not only admiring the growth and potential of others, but also making heroes of them.*

Honesty is aware of limitations. Honesty is not only aware of superpowers, but is also tuned-in to the areas where it falls short (we all do!) and is transparent with others.

Honesty is willing to put others on stage. Honesty does not need or seek the limelight. You can find Honesty in the back of the room not only admiring the growth and potential of others, but also making heroes of them.

It is with this foundation—the commitment to tell the truth and seek the truth in the workplace and one's personal life—that we now delve more deeply into what you are dying to know: *"How can I grow?" and "How can I help others grow?"*

The Path to LIFT

As a business leader, you have an incredible opportunity to create cultures of total growth, starting with a deep-dive focus on the person you are—which, apart from boldness and honesty, is a matter of cultivating what I call "LIFT." My recommendation is that future development plans should incorporate aspects of LIFT, and ultimately focus on your potential as a *whole* person, not just a workplace person.

LIFT is a mnemonic device that serves as an easy-to-remember and easy-to-execute formula. Next, we'll explore each step on the path to LIFT:

L – The letter L in the word LIFT stands for 'love.'

I – The letter I in the word LIFT stands for 'imprint.'

F – The letter F in the word LIFT stands for 'focus.'

T – The letter T in the word LIFT stands for 'time.'

LOVE Imprint Focus Time

Love is the ultimate focal point for the personal growth strategy. It is the intimate circle of people whom you love deeply. Regardless of what kind of growth strategy you are designing, personal or business-related, you need a point of focus. And the focal point has nothing to do with where you're going, what you are going to do, or even what you want to be.

> *When the tough gets going (and it will), what will keep you growing?*

Not even close. The ultimate starting point is "who"—that is, other people.

If your business strategy is built on a target customer that matters to your organization, then your personal growth strategy starts with an intimate circle of people that matter to you. 'Who' is your audience, your tribe, or your customer—the people you love deeply and are most important to you. It can also include your family, your spouse, the team of people you lead at the office, and your friends.

When the tough gets going (and it will), what will keep you growing? During the difficult times, instead of focusing on *what's* at stake, choose to focus on *who's* at stake. The possibility of letting someone down (yourself included) whom you love deeply is everything you need to stay on the climb.

Start with your list of *who*.

Love **IMPRINT** Focus Time

'Imprint' is about being intentional about the kind of fingerprints you leave behind, and how they impact others. To 'imprint' something means to fix indelibly or permanently (as on the memory) or to make a lasting impression or mark on (something or someone).

Imprint is about defining the kind of legacy, lasting impression or mark that you intend to leave on someone's life. I love the word 'imprint' as it makes me think of leaving a thumbprint or fingerprint, unique to only you. You might hear someone say, "His (or her) hand was all over this." Essentially, this means that the person made an impression only he or she could make—unique, like fingerprints.

You can leave your imprint on your children by being an example of the kind of husband or wife your children would ultimately choose. In the workplace, you can care deeply about other people's personal potential and professional growth.

A defined imprint will ultimately dictate how you need to lead your life and, most importantly, will highlight gaps between "who you are" and "who you will become."

Love Imprint **FOCUS** Time

I love the word 'focus'; it's all about simplifying. And hopefully, that equates to simplifying life for you and me, right? 'Focus' in the LIFT acronym is about narrowing efforts to what really matters—which ultimately, as we have established, is the people you love and care about. But 'focus' requires us to hone in on habits and behavior you must commit to developing in order to have the most positive impact on others.

For example, if you wish to influence your children toward a healthy lifestyle, you might need to focus your habit development in the area of fitness and nutrition. Or, if your plan is to influence your staff at the office toward continued learning, you might develop a focus in which you are intentional with specific

> *Only when we focus on the potential of others do we draw closer to our own potential.*

opportunities for development—perhaps even participating alongside them—to really leave a mark.

Love Imprint Focus **TIME**

Essentially, 'time' ties LIFT together: 'Time' encompasses the act of committing to invest a certain amount of your week (say, a minimum of 20 minutes each day for eight weeks) *focused* on one new habit or behavior that will have a potential to impact *(imprint)* someone you care about deeply *(love)*.

LIFT focuses on others. Only when you focus on the potential of others do you draw closer to your own potential.

If you want to create a culture of growth in your organization, you must first realize that a lack of growth in your personal life ultimately impedes progress professionally. Then you must do something about it—which is where LIFT comes in. LIFT is the trigger point for leaders to start building the kind of cultures that perform consistently—growing numbers *and* growing people.

The Second Most Important Day of Your Life

I believe the two most important days in a person's life are the day you were born and the day you discovered *why*.

How many people go through life without discovering the *why*? The leaders of a growth-oriented business culture can honestly say they've answered this question—and ideally, the other team members and employees have, as well. So, what is your "why"?

One of my favorite illustrations of this took place in 1961 when President Kennedy toured the NASA station as crews prepared to attempt the very first trip to the moon. As he walked through the facility, he stopped to speak with a janitor who was mopping floors. When President Kennedy asked the man what he was doing, he replied, "Helping to send a man to the moon!" The man's gift for cleanliness, order, and helping others was passionately

> *Do you know where your unique strengths and gifts intersect with your organization's greatest needs? And where do your greatest strengths and gifts intersect with your team's greatest needs? Shouldn't everybody know the answers to these questions?*

employed to make possible a bigger mission to launch a spaceship.

Purpose and vision function as the spark plug for your personal engine, and they have a chain-reaction effect on absolutely all growth areas of your life, including your business. This is far from a matter of developing a purpose or vision for your life, your family, or your organization and much more about how to *activate* it—which is always the harder part.

Many organizations' efforts to establish purpose and vision can be well-intentioned and inspiring at the start, but ultimately never reach deep enough to stir the passion pools of the individual worker. They fail to catalyze or spark even an ounce of forward-motion, much less the thought of improving engagement (corporate buzzword for 'passion').

The way to fan the spark into a flame is to help *individuals* uncover their "why" and link it to the *organization's* "why." Do you know where your unique strengths and gifts intersect with your organization's greatest needs? And where do your greatest strengths and gifts intersect with your team's greatest needs? Shouldn't *everybody* know the answers to these questions?

Every single person on the planet should have the incredible fortune to know "why," but many do not. We are all born with a deeply wired need to create value for others in our lives and in the lives of others—including our families, our teams, our organizations, and our customers. What this means is that we each know (or discover) precisely the special gifts and strengths God has given us and how those unique strengths add value to a bigger purpose in our lives. In the words of Paul the Apostle, "There are different gifts, but the same Spirit distributes them" (1 Corinthians 12:4 NIV).

With this mindset, dive deep into your own passion pools. If you believe in the power of prayer (I do!), pray about it daily. Where would God have you be/serve/work in a way that you could glorify Him with your gifts and talents? Pray for your children—that they too, would come to know and pursue God's will for their life—that God would use you and your family to impact and reach His people.

> **How about you? What's your "why"?**

Dive deep into the passion pools of your staff. Make certain they are dialed into how their unique strengths and gifts intersect with the organization's purpose and vision.

Help them discover the "why" in their lives. It will be a day they will never forget.

How about you? What's your "why"?

Learn from the Eagle

I find the example of the eagle especially powerful for creating a purposeful, vision-oriented culture of growth. Begin by imagining that you're standing on the roof of a ten-story building. If you had the vision or eyesight of an eagle, you could see an ant crawling on the ground. From its perch at the top of trees or in flight, an eagle can catch sight of a rabbit up to two miles away.

And, when the eagle is ready to dive after its prey, it will reach speeds of 125 to 200 mph while maintaining laser-like control and accuracy of its talons to catch moving objects.

What can leaders learn from the eagle?

What's more, eagles can rotate their heads 270 degrees to see prey or competitors (for the prey) in all directions. Add to all of that a regular cruising flight of 15,000 feet (which is half the altitude of a soaring 757 airplane) and it's easy to see how the eagle is one of the most impressively gifted specimens on planet earth—as well as why it has become synonymous with strength, vision, and essentially everything that constitutes great leadership.

Imagine a single organization or a person possessing an eagle-like arsenal of skills—vision, speed, and execution—all at the same time. Superman in the flesh, right? A combination of those skills would be almost as rare and unstoppable as the eagle itself.

Since most of us don't possess superpowers to effortlessly maneuver our organizations at jet-like speed, is there anything at all about the eagle that you and I, as leaders, can emulate?

Where Is Your Beak Pointing?

Ultimately, however, the eagle's status as a symbol leadership rests on more than how far it sees, how high it soars, and how fast it dives from the sky. The eagle's vision wouldn't matter as much except for this basic, crucial fact: the eagle spends more time with its head *out* of the nest than it does *in* it. The real reason the eagle sees and soars so far is that it has the courage to "point its beak" *outward*.

> *At some point, as we grow older, we stop being curious. And, ultimately, we stop growing.*

And this lesson from the eagle offers real world connection to your leadership potential in the marketplace, if embraced.

Too many of us have our heads down as we run our organizations. We fail to stop, look up and see what's going on around us. It's only when we courageously stick our heads "out of the nest" that we will be able to build our organizations. I call this "outward curiosity."

The discipline of outward curiosity is vital to unleashing new growth in your organization—so, watch the eagle. Building an organizational culture of growth doesn't require you to achieve speeds of 200 mph or a binocular-like sight into the future; rather, it's the simple discipline of lifting your head and "pointing your beak" outward. For it's when you lift your head from the nest that you will find your vision.

Curiosity Stretches Potential

When we stop being curious, we stop growing.

Eagles aren't they only constructive examples of curiosity-driven growth, however. In fact, you need look no farther than our children and a cartoon monkey.

Every morning, after my oldest children get on the bus for school, my youngest daughter loves to watch *Cu-*

rious George. Until it's time to leave for pre-school, she runs off and tries to emulate George through playtime.

Do you remember George? How about the Man with the Yellow Hat? Each episode features that relentless little monkey lured toward some discovery or adventure, often times resulting in temporary chaos. But the story always ends with George having learned or mastered a new skill.

At some point, as we grow older, we stop being curious. And, ultimately, we stop growing.

Essentially, we stop stretching on purpose, only to find ourselves gradually drifting further away from the edges of our comfort zone. Instead of allowing ourselves to be lured to discovery, we are lulled to sleep. Companies, leaders and the people who work for them must be unwilling to stop learning. They must never stop growing. Like George, they must never stop discovering new things and being curious!

> *All great strategies were devised as a result of a new discovery.*

All great strategies were devised as a result of a new discovery. If you haven't yet, you must implement an annual, deep-dive exploration strategy (a scuba dive, not a surface snorkel) for you and your staff to include some of the following areas:

You must become intently curious about your employee performers. Don't forget to seek their input!

- To deliver real long-term value, how will you cultivate the kind of culture that has employees bringing their very best self to work each and every day?

- What are three ways you can help each employee (individually) grow personally?

You must also become curious about the end consumer. Everything starts with the consumers' needs and wants, so you need to get to the roots—even if it gets a little messy. To deliver real long-term value, ask yourself:

> *You need to be serving a market as well as creating a new market at all times.*

- What are the top three expressed and unexpressed needs she or he has?
- How does the consumer ultimately choose your product or service, and how does he or she use it?

You must become curious about the edges of your marketplace. You need to be serving a market as well as creating a new market at all times. Most likely, your new market will be a result of some new discovery you make through the exploration.

- Have you challenged your team to go deep in understanding the market in which you compete today as well as the one you will build tomorrow?

You must become curious about the trends you missed as well as upcoming trends and how they will impact your business. As cliché as it might be, trends are like waves; while you ride one today, position yourself for the next one tomorrow.

- What three trends could you have a team start working on tomorrow?

So, before you leave for work one morning this week, spend five extra minutes with your son and/or daughter, watching a little *Curious George*. And then, run off to the office to emulate George. You will be amazed with new discoveries and what they might mean for your growth strategy. Consider, too, bringing in a professional "Curious George"—partnering with an expert advisor in growth from outside your organization. Such a person will challenge and stretch your thinking in new ways— not only from the right data and insight, but also from experience.

Your Words: Curiosity Killers or Growth Engines?

Your words bear fruit—hopefully good fruit.

Constructive curiosity is inextricably tied to innovation in your organization's culture. Innovation also happens to be one of the biggest present-day challenges for organizations of all sizes. In fact, a large number (65% or more) cite innovation to be one of their toughest strategic challenges. Yet, if you get it right, innovative companies, on average, grow 13 percent annually as compared to other companies, whose growth hovers around 5 percent. Even more compellingly, the five-year compounded growth rates of innovative companies are 84 percent as compared to 28 percent for all the rest.

Isn't it worth your time to look closely at the barriers to innovation that obstruct your organization's path to growth?

> *Our words do one of two things: they either build up or tear down. It's our choice.*

One of the questions executives ask me most often is "How can we encourage creativity and build an innovative culture across all functions?" One of the first steps in fostering this kind of culture in your organization is for you to take the "brutally honest" mirror test.

As leaders, I don't think we realize the impact our word choice (as well as our body language) has on our teams and the people with whom we interact daily. When we inadvertently shut down ideas and creativity through our language (both spoken and unspoken), it's highly likely our people will stop producing fruit altogether. Growth will be stifled dramatically. When this happens, it's like life being sucked out of a tree that has not been watered. And a dead tree bears no fruit.

Don't let this happen on your watch. Our words do one of two things: they either build up or tear down. It's our choice.

In our company, we often conduct brainstorming sessions to address business model innovation with clients. Prior to kick-off, we typically establish pre-session guidelines that include removing word phrases that tend to close doors and replacing those words with "open door" phrases that encourage the flow of ideas.

Here are five examples:

- Instead of saying, "We've tried that before," try *"There's always room for improvement!"*
- Instead of saying, "It's alright in theory," try *"Think of the possibilities!"*
- Instead of saying, "It's too radical of a change," try *"Let's hear more ideas on that topic."*
- Instead of saying, "It's too complicated and difficult," try *"We can be the first!"*
- Instead of saying, "It's too risky," try *"How might we learn more about that idea and its impact on ____?"*

The idea is to change the language, and the tone of the language, from the top down. Word choice is a small step forward in turning a business culture in the right direction. Word choice and tone will reverberate and domino through the organization. The impact is what matters.

Everyone is designed with an inherent drive to create or add value. When you—the leader—open the door and encourage the flow of ideas, watch the fruit grow!

So, let me ask you to be brutally honest on this topic: What kind of wake are you leaving behind you when the meeting concludes? After the doors close and the teams disperse to their cubicles, are they inspired to dig deeper into their creative wells to solve problems, or are they parched, withered, and shut down?

> *After the doors close and the teams disperse to their cubicles, are they inspired to dig deeper into their creative wells to solve problems, or are they parched, withered, and shut down?*

The late Robin Williams said it best: "No matter what people tell you, words and ideas can change the world."[5]

It's a choice we are privileged to make.

Think back to the child-like curiosity of Curious George. Children exemplify what it's like to live in the moment—to just *be*. Leaving what *was* or what's *next* in favor of what *is*, with the brimming courage to be seen exactly for who they are.

So, how often do you find yourself in-the-moment, unencumbered by what was, or what's next? Change your word choice and you just might change the way you answer this question.

It Starts with a Circle

In the business world, growth is often compared to ascending a mountain, constructing a building, or climbing a ladder.

As an entrepreneur focused on continual growth, the frustration I've always had with mountains is that they never get discernably higher. Once you climb to the top, the journey is over, right?

When construction ends on a building, the trucks eventually leave the site. Once the project is complete, nothing more happens until everything starts to look outdated in twenty years. In business, this concept is referred to as the proverbial ladder-to-the-top that says, "You can only climb so high before you need to start adding rungs."

However, instead of climbing or building, what if there were a better model for an organizational culture of *ongoing* growth—one that would reflect consistent forward progress? For this, you need a **circle**.

Think about the seasons of the year—they are unstoppable. Each year, predictably, your infant bushes and trees grow wider and taller. Spring follows the darkness of winter, without anyone planning it. Flowers bud, and grass turns green again. Soon summer follows, and before you know it, the leaves are turning colors, welcoming fall.

What if you generated that kind of steady, repeatable, predictable growth year in and year out in all aspects of your *life*?

At the heart of every great growth story is a circle containing a big, bold dream, with lots of smaller circles clustered around it.

In business, your circle can be your direction, your team, your strategy, your process, your prayer, and ultimately, your impact. It can be your business organization's culture as a whole, and it can shape your growth, starting today.

The bottom line is this: you only have two options.

In any given moment we have two options: to step forward into growth or to step back into safety. — **Abraham Maslow**[6]

Now let's consider the image of the circle in a different way: at the heart of every great growth story is a circle containing a big, bold dream, with lots of smaller circles clustered around it. Unmet potential is commonplace in businesses everywhere because, whether it be obstacles, artificial limitations, distractions or fear, the small circles sometimes swallow the big.

However, if you surround yourself with the right partners, the right people, and the right strategy, you can confidently pursue the big growth goals in your central circle.

So, what's in your circle? What big business and people-building dreams are front and center in your life? Ultimately, it's up to you to step forward—or should I say *circle* forward—and begin to grow!

WORKBOOK

Chapter 1 Questions

Question: As a business leader, what are you curious about? What should you be curious about? What is one step you can take to promote a culture of curiosity and open communication within your organization?

_____

_____

_____

_____

_____

_____

_____

_____

_____

_____

_____

Question: What growth-friendly language do you employ? List three to four ways you will be more growth-friendly in your language and tone when communicating with your leadership team and employees.

_____

_____

_____

_____

_____

_____

_____

_____

_____

_____

_____

_____

_____

_____

Question: What does the LIFT model mean to you personally? Think of one person (team member, direct report, son or daughter, etc.) with whom you will apply the LIFT model. Who is it? How will you apply each of the steps (Love, Imprint, Focus, Time)?

_____

_____

_____

_____

_____

_____

_____

_____

_____

_____

_____

_____

_____

_____

_____

Circle Back: Foster a culture of growth in your organization by growing personally and maintaining a passionate focus on the people you care about—from your family and friends to your customers and team members. Address growth challenges by promoting honesty and accountability and by remaining curious and open to new ideas and information. To this end, use growth-friendly language to encourage honest, open communication. As a leader, commit yourself to the LIFT path—Love, Imprint, Focus, and Time—so that you, and your organization as a whole, will be equipped to achieve continuous growth. Remember, all sustained growth is circular—not linear. Here's to climbing circles rather than mountains!

CHAPTER TWO

Grow into Overdrive:
Developing Growth-Oriented Strategy

Two brands, both lagging. One of those brands decided it was time to grow. The other brand decided to design and build an icon.

Both brands announced innovations that would deliver a higher level of value and consumer experience never before seen in their respective markets.

They both raised the bar for their industries and did so with an extensive understanding of the consumers they serve—including understanding their unmet desires, as well as their real competitors.

Because of this innovation, these two brands will never be the same. So, who are these come-from-behind brands?

One is Motorola—yes, Motorola, which announced an entire new family of high-performing, innovative products in the "Moto" line, including the Moto Hint and Moto 360, at a private event. Moto Hint allowed consumers complete control of their smartphones through an ear bud, and the use of only their voice. The much anticipated Moto 360 was a beautifully designed, round-faced smartwatch with a custom leather band. The Moto 360 sold out almost immediately.

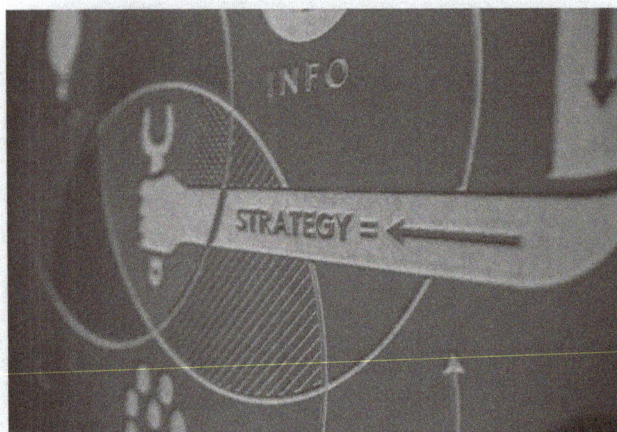

How strong are your strategic thinking skills?

A second brand that came from behind is a pro football team—the Atlanta Falcons. In 2013 the Atlanta Falcons unveiled the design details behind their brand new, $1.2 billion stadium. Prior to announcing these detailed plans, however, the Falcons were immersed in an intricate "possibilities thinking" process. They dove deep into creating a complete experience that would move consumers to leave the confines of their comfy homes, iPads, and fancy TVs to make the trip to see the sport live.

In particular, I love how the Falcons' organization and ownership embarked on the stadium project—their ambition was to create and build an icon for the city, the sport, and even broader, the world.

And this step-out came from a lower-profile professional sports town where a large percentage of residents hail from other cities or favor SEC college football over the NFL.

So, in thinking about strategy development, first consider what icons you are building right now, either in your personal life or within your business. Where do you need to raise the bar? How can you consider bigger "what if" possibilities?

This might just be the kind of push-to-the-edge strategic thinking that has the power to change your life, your business, and your customers' world.

Feeling Stuck?

Let's be honest, nearly every great business leader I have met admits to having been "stuck" at some point in his or her business pursuits. Maybe you're thinking of starting a business. Or you've started a business, but progress is slow or has stalled. Perhaps you have been in a family or founder-led business for a lengthy period of time and are experiencing another plateau of little to no growth. Maybe you are primed and ready for expansion into new channels, markets, or products.

In all cases, you may find yourself frustrated or stuck, exploring options, and trying to establish clarity and focus on what to do next. There is no better way to become "unstuck" than to clarify your business strategy.

Let this chapter be the tow-truck-solution right when you need it most—providing insight and direction on how to propel your business forward. Forward movement is the outcome of a growth-oriented culture, as we saw in Chapter 1, but forward movement also results when a strong, growth-oriented business strategy is in place. Strategy and culture are mutually reinforcing: if you are successful in laying the right strategy and cultivating the right culture, the outcome will naturally be growth.

> *Strategy and culture are mutually reinforcing: if you are successful in laying the right strategy and cultivating the right culture, the outcome will naturally be growth.*

But first you must be willing to dig past the painful symptoms of being stuck in a rut and instead address the root problems.

Your Pain Is a Symptom of a Much Bigger Problem

Pain tells a story. About six years ago, severe lower back pain brought me to my knees like an unearthed oak tree in a tornado.

I suffered what would become a string of painful and debilitating periods where I would scratch and claw to get back on my feet, throwing anything I could at the pain, from heat, to ice, to bottles of ibuprofen and aspirin.

The pain would eventually subside and I would return to my normal schedule only to be blitzed again with the same pain a few short months later.

I quickly became tired and frustrated of trying to treat symptoms. Learning that back pain was very common in men and that surgery is only an option in severe cases, I ultimately discovered the underlying problem stemmed from a weak midsection and tight hamstring muscles.

> *The lack of innovation within your organization is a symptom of a much bigger problem. The problem is a weak strategy.*

Once I attacked the deeper problem, my back pain was a distant memory.

Lack of innovation, if not addressed, can have a similar impact on your business' long-term health, leading to painful and debilitating periods of customer defect and flat to no sales growth.

A compelling infographic featured in an Inc.com summer article, "The Innovation Strategies that Lead to Success," highlights the following:

Sixty-one percent of companies cite innovation as a major focus within their businesses, yet 55 percent don't seek out innovation opportunities and an astounding 66 percent do not have well-defined innovation strategies. Perhaps most impacting, innovative companies, on average, grow 13 percent annually as compared to other companies who grew only five percent. The five-year compounded growth rate of innovative companies is 84 percent as compared to 28 percent of all the rest![7]

Here is the brutally honest headline:

The lack of innovation within your organization is a symptom of a much bigger problem. *The problem is a weak strategy.*

Consider whether the following occur in your company:

- Are your employee teams challenged to describe, very specifically, your target consumer or customer?
- Do your employees give different answers when asked to articulate your core value proposition?
- How frequently (if ever) do your marketing teams leave the office, spending time in the market with your end-user?
- Does leadership spend too much time assessing the competition and not enough time assessing your customers' needs?
- Is your business managed with a short-term sense of urgency in making numbers, resulting in flavor-of-the-month changes in direction?
- Is decision-making sluggish rather than crisp, with a clear strategy?
- Are your budget dollars allocated too evenly across a wide portfolio, geared at numerous small, meaningless innovation projects and leaving few to no dollars for bigger breakthrough work?

- Is there a debilitating fear of failure running rampant in your organization rather than a circular, iterative process that fosters a build–test–learn–refine approach?

Were your answers to the above questions surprising? Revealing?

If so, the underlying problem is either a weak strategy or a complete lack of strategy. And, without a strategy, you're unlikely to have structured your teams correctly and therefore, lack the underpinnings for a solid culture that can drive the processes needed to spark breakthrough innovation.

Eradicate the underlying problem and the symptoms disappear. Permanently.

Next, let's consider several ways to transform your business strategy.

Four Questions That Will Reframe Your Strategy

Let's dig into four questions that, over the course of this chapter, will reframe how you approach your strategy:

1. Who are we?

This question is designed for you to describe who you are—your values, your story, and your identity. Tell me about *you*—as a person or business—your heritage, your history, events that have marked your life or business, and the values that define how you live, work, and play.

Next, tell your story. Your story should illuminate to your customers why you are doing what you are doing. Give me reasons to believe in your cause. Everybody's story is unique and must be brought to the surface in your business strategy so your customers can feel your passion bleeding through everything you do, create, and deliver to the marketplace.

2. Whom do we serve?

We all serve others. Whether as parents at home serving our children, the homeowner needing new light fixtures installed, or the company needing safety training for all their manufacturing plants, we *serve* people. This question works as it drives focus on users and real people, not heavy demographics and statistics.

All growth strategies primarily start from the customer (those being served) and should be heavily connected to your identity.

You need to have a high-definition picture of exactly whom you serve through your business offering and where you can find your customer. Essentially, in what industry, market, and geography do you compete? Make a check-box list that describes your customers inside and out—exactly how your customers think and feel, their problems, their needs, and their dreams.

3. What value do we add?

The value you add is an intersection. It's where your unique strengths collide with the unique needs of those you serve. This question helps you keep rooted in creating value for others, while continuing to test, assess, and enhance that value offering. There are gaps in the marketplace, as defined by your customers, and your charge is to uncover those gaps and design a proposition that plugs the hole. Everyone is wired to create value for others and experience the feeling that comes from the act of creating value for others.

When considering what value your organization adds, it is helpful to describe *how* the value you add will impact your customer when done right. Describe how your end user will feel and act, how your product or service might change them for the better, and how you envision your customers sharing their experience with others.

> *Failure to align the strategy of the organization closely to its current stage of growth will undoubtedly result in underperformance, ultimately putting your place in the market at great risk.*

4. How will we do it?

Assessing how your organization does what it does forces you to think about the capabilities you will need to deliver your value to the marketplace. Some capabilities may already exist and some may need to be added. Most likely, your capabilities will be unique to your organization, product or service and divergent from your competitive set. Most importantly, your organization's key capabilities will be exactly what is required to bring your value proposition to life for the customers whom you serve.

What elements help you deliver your end product or result to the customer? You may identify elements such as your go-to-market strategy, buying process, acquisition strategy, or even major initiatives with respect to your team members as capabilities that help you deliver on your promises.

If you journey through the four questions above correctly, you and your team should feel impassioned, confident, and focused when finished! The result will be clarity and a deeper conviction of who you are, whom you serve, the value you add, and how you bring it to life. What could be more energizing?

Do You Know What Stage Your Business Is In?

Once you've defined who you are as a business, whom you serve, and the value you add, it's critical to assess the stage of your business. So, what stage is your business in right now? Let's take a look...

Figure 2.1 below as an example to illustrate four possible stages (with hypothetical sales volumes) in which a business might progress over time. Businesses of all sizes and industries advance through different stages of growth that require deliberate thought and planning with respect to strategy.

+ Business Stages
Aligning Your Strategy to Your Stage

Stage:	Introduction Stage: 0 – 10m	Growth Stage: 10 – 50m	Expansion Stage: 50 – 100m	Maturity Stage: 100m+
Strategy:	Traction	Existing Market	New Markets	New Products/ Services
Structure:	Speed	Sales	Service	Specialized
Talent:	Passionate	Creative	Collaborative	Innovative
Process:	Test	Scale	Refine	Adapt

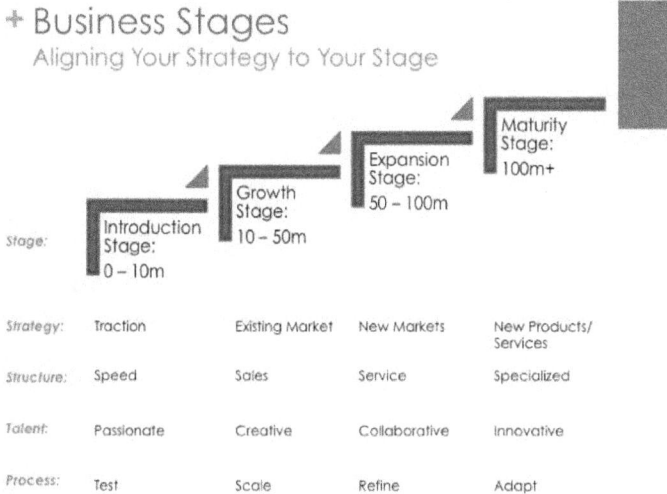

Figure 2.1: Business Stages

Failure to align the strategy of the organization closely to its current stage of growth will undoubtedly result in underperformance, ultimately putting your place in the market at great risk. In the example above, a growth-stage business that prematurely decides to reduce headcount in a sales function in favor of building efficiencies for expansion-stage will negatively impact its market share in existing markets.

Conversely, the same is true of the organization that fails to staff adequately toward efficiency as expansion occurs to new markets. The strategy is at risk due to the organization's inability to establish awareness and meet customer demand in new markets. Ideally, this is not the kind of first impression you want to deliver as you move from existing markets to new markets.

Four Business Growth Stages

| Introduction | Growth | Expansion | Maturity |

Introduction Stage. In the introduction stage, an organization has developed a product or service that it's bringing to a target audience and market. The strategy in this particular stage typically entails a smaller team of passionate visionaries who are aggressively promoting their brand to establish quick traction. The business is structured very loosely and somewhat decentralized, allowing the team the ability to respond to opportunity quickly as well as the flexibility to make adjustments as the learning process unfolds.

| Introduction | → | Growth | → | Expansion | → | Maturity |

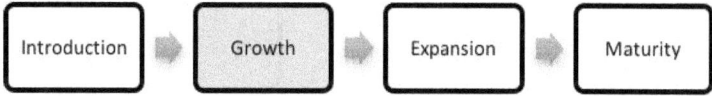

Growth Stage. As a business gains traction, its primary market, audience, and competition for the product or service will begin to crystallize. When this occurs, it's time for the business to begin modifying its strategy to align with the growth stage. The strategy can more specifically center on deeply penetrating the primary market with an increased sales and marketing presence. As the business grows, talent requirements change. It's necessary to have creative business builders who can begin to scale the messaging, awareness, and engagement for the products. It's not entirely out of the question to see organizations bring close-to-the-core product innovation to market late in the growth stage (service enhancements, version updates, new colors or variations), although true white-space innovation takes a backseat until later.

| Introduction | → | Growth | → | Expansion | → | Maturity |

Expansion Stage. Typically, an organization will know it's time to move into the expansion stage when it experiences its first significant plateau event. Toward the end of the growth stage, businesses will start to press up against the ceiling in the primary market. Commonly, moving into the expansion stage might consist of bringing new products to primary markets or introducing your primary product to new markets. In this example, I suggest that you evaluate a new market move first, as advancing to new product (or category) development requires a more specialized structure and talent profile.

A new market expansion strategy will often require some staffing adjustments in order to become more collaborative and service-oriented while ensuring the ability to respond to new target audience needs, but you're in a strong position with a proven, profitable product or service that has been perfected in primary market learning.

Introduction		Growth		Expansion		Maturity

Maturity Stage. In the latter half of the expansion stage, organizations might experience increased competition, new entrants, or other external challenges that will often lead to another plateau event signaling the onset of the maturity stage. From the latter half of the expansion stage to the beginning of maturity, organizations must be engaging deeper with their target audience to build an innovation strategy. Bringing new products and services to market (whether expansion to new categories with in-house talent or via acquisition) is vital to your survival.

In general, with strong analytics and an internal growth strategy system that drives the day-to-day business, leadership should be in position to stay in front of the stages, preparing their organizations for a running start through possible plateaus lingering on the horizon. Making the proper changes and adjustments too late in a particular stage can have a lasting impact on your business.

This happens to be one of those unique opportunities—a chance to step back and ask a few critical questions before dialing-in your strategy for the upcoming year. Ask yourself:

- What stage is your business in currently? Have you aligned your strategy, structure, talent and process to cater to that particular stage?
- If you're experiencing one of those plateaus referenced above, what adjustments need to occur to blast through it?
- What preparations need to happen now in order to be ready for the next stage on the horizon?

When it comes to the latter two questions, it's especially helpful to reflect in detail on the people your business serves—the customers. Let's turn, then, to the customer experience and the concept of adding value.

The Customer Experience: Building a Path to Spectacular

For the last several years, we have reserved our children's spring break week for Disney World in Orlando, Florida. A favorite experience, without question, was the nightly fireworks display over the castle in the main park— even though it made for a late night for the kids.

> *When products and services are easily copied, experiences differentiate.*

It's always interesting to see other families' memories being made at Disney World throughout the year, proudly recorded on Facebook and other social media venues.

It's where memories are made—and shared—with millions! In response to those posts and pictures come "likes" and comments from those who have never been to Disney and dream of going, as well as those who want to return.

Build a path to spectacular!

This is how "spectacular" works.

In the book *Be Our Guest*, the Disney Institute and Theodore Kinni cite a 70 percent customer return rate, which is remarkably high for a theme park.[8] While certainly overused for illustrating outstanding customer experience practices, Disney never ceases to inspire, from every angle.

Why couldn't your business be more Disney-like?

If a strategy, at its core, is about defining your customer, the value you deliver that customer, and how you deliver it in the marketplace, then "experience" matters.

Additionally, when products and services are easily copied, *experiences* differentiate. I suggest that *experience* innovation be one of your top five growth initiatives each year—given the fast changes occurring in technology.

There are three very easy questions that your marketing, customer experience, or service teams should be pondering at every touch point with your customers. If you have never considered a path-to-purchase or consumer journey project within your organization, this is a perfect time.

> **What emotions and feelings are your customer interactions generating?**

A consumer journey map defines the end-to-end path a customer follows from (1) first awareness of your product or brand(s) to (b) how he or she seeks product information, (c) how he or she interacts with your technology, your social media and your employees, and ultimately, (d) how the customer makes the final purchasing decision.

Emotional feelings lead to rational thoughts and rational thoughts will drive or elicit some kind of response or action on the part of your customer. To the best of your ability, the charge is to own this chain reaction at every step, turn and interaction on the journey.

What emotions and feelings are your customer interactions generating? Define exactly how you want your consumer or customer to feel when they drive into your parking lot(s) or use your bathrooms. How do customers feel after interacting with your customer service staff or team members? What opinions are your customers forming as a result of those feelings?

If emotions and feelings drive rational thoughts, then what rational conclusions might the customer make about the attention to detail in your restaurant if the restroom is dirty or if the paper towel roll is empty? If your website interface is confusing and difficult to navigate, what questions might that trigger in the customer's mind regarding your business's ability to deliver results in a predictable or comprehensible manner? What actions might the customer take as a result?

> *No action is sometimes a signal that the customer experience broke down at some point in the process.*

Will the emotions and thoughts your customers experience drive them to act in your favor or in opposition? In other words, will they click "purchase" or will they "abandon"? Will they "share"? Will they "return again"? Or will they simply do nothing? No action is sometimes a signal that the customer experience broke down at some point in the process.

> *The spectacular is shared and experienced over and over again.*

So, will you consider mapping a path-to-purchase for your brand? But don't stop at the purchase. I encourage you to go beyond the tangible transaction (where most organizations stop).

Challenge yourself to build a path to the *spectacular*, as Disney does. The *spectacular* is shared and experienced over and over again.

If you are failing to achieve the spectacular, or the kind of traction you desire with your business, you may be plugged into the wrong source for growth. Identifying where you will source your growth is one of the most commonly missed steps in designing the right strategy for your business.

Unfortunately, if you fail to get it right, it can have lasting repercussions on how you define and deliver value to your target customer.

A critical exercise in the early stages of building a strong strategy is to declare the market in which you intend to source growth. Evaluate the opportunities you may be missing that could create new or better value for a target customer. This kind of analysis begins to lift the fog and provide clarity as to the winning value proposition you can use across your brand marketing, product development and execution in the market.

There is no shortage of companies that have identified the right market sources for their future growth. Here are just a few examples:

Sonos: Bring all your music to every room, wirelessly.

Sonos clearly identified the wired speaker market as a source for growth and designed a value proposition that delivered the first wireless solution to the consumer who loves music. For customers who listen to music through a tuner and components system, delivering sound via wired speakers in ceilings and walls, Sonos was, literally, music to their ears—wirelessly.

Dyson Airblade: No more waste, no restocking, and no paper mess.

Dyson identified the commercial restroom paper towel and dispenser market as a source for growth by leveraging their technology to create a revolutionary (better) way to dry hands after washing. If you've never used a Dyson Airblade, prepare yourself to experience some serious air flow—not to mention a visit to a clean bathroom with no paper mess.

Uber: Your shortcut to everywhere is arriving now.

Uber was clear about putting a stake in the transportation market as a primary source for growth. Uber improved the overall experience of getting a ride wherever you are and whenever you want—hence the "shortcut." You can literally watch your car on your smartphone as it arrives to pick you up.

Microsoft Surface Pro 3: The tablet that can replace your laptop.

Just another tablet, right? Wrong. The Surface Pro is not aimed at winning market share in the tablet market (however, that may be a future by-product). Instead, Microsoft seeks to source its growth from the laptop market. When the original Surface Pro was launched, it was quickly lumped into a growing tablet market—along with Apple and Samsung—and did not possess a distinct value proposition or sharp messaging to "win" in the right market. The recent launch of Surface Pro 3 brings a much sharper value proposition to the marketplace, and consequently, the sales have been much stronger.

As the preceding examples illustrate, the markets in which you choose to participate ultimately provide clarity in building the right value proposition.

If you put a stake in the right market, it has the power to change everything—including entire industries.

Value Proposition: A Necessary Key

Let's now turn to your organization's value proposition. First, what is it? In a nutshell, a value proposition is a promise of value to be delivered. It's the primary reason a prospect should buy from you. A value proposition:

- explains how your product solves customers' problems or improves their lives;

- delivers specific benefits;

- tells your customers why they should buy from you rather than from the competition.

Perhaps you are contemplating market expansion for your organization, but aren't sure how to get access and traction with your product or service. Or maybe you've expanded to a new market recently, but are not yet resonating with your target audience.

When asked, "What do you do?" or "How are you different?" do you find that your sales, service and marketing teams all have different answers or responses—almost as if they were singing out of tune? If any of the above resonates, chances are your value proposition needs work.

> *Your value proposition is also the key that unlocks focus, passion, and engagement in your people—if communicated and cascaded through the organization correctly.*

Sonos, Dyson Airblade, Uber, and Microsoft Surface Pro 3 were all able to identify and create a value proposition that delighted their customers—and the result is success in their markets. A strong value proposition is the key that unlocks the door to new markets. And with many businesses seeking to grow by expanding to new markets or appealing to new customer segments, there may be no topic more important than how to develop a strong value proposition.

In addition, I would suggest that your value proposition is also the key that unlocks focus, passion, and engagement in your people—if communicated and cascaded through the organization correctly. If you believe you have a strong value proposition but have not gained the traction you thought you might, it could be that your organization needs to re-evaluate its value proposition.

Let's unpack the major components of a solid value proposition.

Value Proposition Map

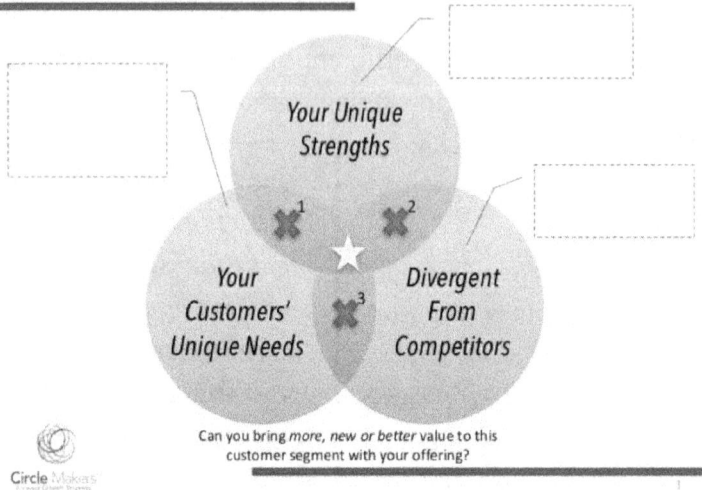

Your Unique
Strengths

Your
Customers'
Unique Needs

Divergent
From
Competitors

Can you bring *more, new or better* value to this
customer segment with your offering?

Circle Makers

Figure 2.2: Value Proposition Map

Circle 1: Your Unique Strengths

Figure 2.2 is a value proposition map my firm utilizes with our clients. It's a simple Venn diagram designed to provide clarity as you find your "sweet spot" within a particular market or with a certain audience. The blank box connected to each circle offers space to begin writing out relevant details and ideas.

I highly recommend you start your value proposition work in the "Unique Strengths" circle. Here's why: as you consider moving into new markets or generating appeal with a new audience, it's critical you lead from a position of strength.

Picture your brand or business as an arrow flying into a new market toward a target. The sharpest part of the arrow should be the core strength in your offering. The balance of the arrow can be comprised of capabilities considered necessary, or required, as part of new market entry.

An exercise that might precede your analysis of "unique strengths" is a simple SWOT analysis assessing your organization's Strengths, Weaknesses, Opportunities, and Threats. You'll want to identify the special strengths or capabilities you possess, have built or are currently building that address a specific problem you seek to solve. For example, strengths or capabilities might surface in the form of intellectual property, technologies, infrastructure, or talent.

Circle 2: Your Customers' Unique Needs

This circle requires some upfront research to understand your target audience more fully. It's much deeper and more holistic than simply knowing what problem your audience has that your offering solves. Understanding the motivations, emotions, and frustration the problem creates in your target audience's lives is also a critical learning at this stage.

As you work within this circle, it's important to ensure you have a good handle on the real problem you're trying to solve for the target audience. Within the vast digital landscape, there are numerous tools available to help you better understand your target audience. An obvious strategy is to speak directly with your target audience or prospect to uncover potential gaps or unmet needs that exist.

Circle 3: Divergent from Your Competitors

The third and final circle in our model also requires research and understanding of the competitive offerings in the marketplace to ensure your offering is not an exact match with someone else's offering. Having two brands or businesses in the same market with the same offering will only detract from your efforts.

More than ever, the big ideas that deliver big value are happening at the hands of partnerships.

Understanding the competitive marketplace landscape can help you prioritize potential sweet spots for your unique offering. Who competes in the space? How well do they address the top needs of this target audience? Where are the gaps within the current offerings?

Strategic Partnerships

As we've noted, while you certainly must be aware of the competition, not every organization relevant to your business needs to be viewed as a competitor.

Strategic alliances are best formed with a dual-sided intent to create more, new, and/or better value for customers through a new innovation. More than ever, the *big* ideas that deliver *big* value are happening at the hands of partnerships.

There is no better example of this principle in action than Delta Airlines. Several years ago, Delta Airlines announced it was launching a mentorship program, in partnership with LinkedIn, designed to connect professionals flying via Delta Airlines. By targeting the working (and traveling) professional, the Delta brand enhanced the customer experience by creating a stronger "community" amongst the several thousand professionals who fly their airline every day. For the traveling professional, this community creates a reason to fly Delta. Additionally, the program bridges the digital and physical worlds of LinkedIn and Delta. Appropriately referred to as "Innovation Class," the program will be something the weary traveler who has been on one too many flights will appreciate.

If strategic partnerships can succeed within an airline, chances are great that they can work in virtually any business. Here are two questions to prompt your thinking regarding how partnerships might benefit your organization and, ultimately, add more value for your customers:

1. Where are the holes in your offering or your service and who can plug them? When combined, does the mutual value created provide both companies access to a bigger market that you previously could not access individually?
2. In your market, where is there an opportunity to combine forces and build large-scale momentum in order to deliver new value, where everyone wins? Delta and LinkedIn are a great example.

Real innovation in the air (literally)! Makes you kind of forget about baggage fees, and better snacks and drinks, doesn't it?

Your Customer's Purchase Journey

Chances are, you're outfitted with a world class Customer Relationship Management (CRM) software. A super-sized, gazillion dollar industry has led to more collaboration, real-time information and analytics that businesses everywhere hope to leverage with the goal of driving revenue.

But, is your CRM platform working for you? If not, *why not?*

CRM systems have greatly enhanced organizations' capacity (or lack thereof) to build, execute, and track the process in which they advance customers through different sales and service funnels or stages. While these processes are designed to drive an outcome for the organization, they often fail to take into account the customer's purchase journey.

Below we will review two crucial steps toward making this critical shift.

1. Understand the stages of your customer's purchase journey.

Do you know the stages your customers experience when purchasing your product or service? Most importantly, do you know what your customer needs to feel comfortable continuing to the next stage in their purchasing journey? The majority of organizations have a difficult time answering these questions—you're not alone! The customer journey map (Figure 2.3 below) is the most effective way to understand your customer's purchasing process. The first column of the table below identifies generic customer stages.

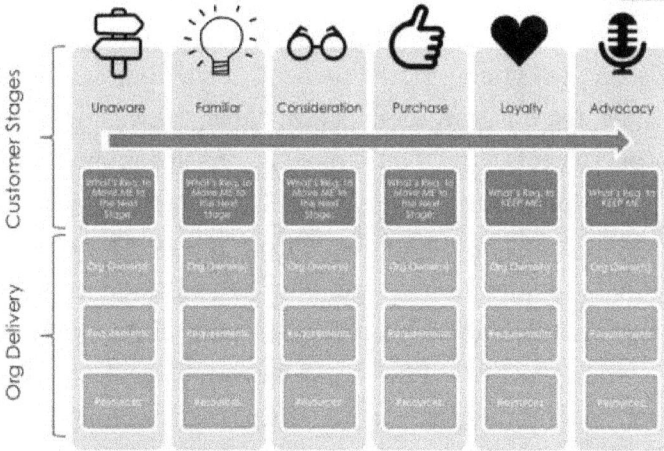

Figure 2.3: Customer Journey Map

The second column poses questions about your objective with respect to the customer at each stage. Here you define what your business must do in order for your customer to feel comfortable enough to advance to the next stage. Additionally, if you've done the proper research on your customer's purchase journey, you should understand the emotional response you are striving to create.

2. Align your organizational delivery to the customer purchase journey

The third column of Figure 2.3 identifies several categories of "organizational delivery" for each customer stage: (a) one or more "owners," or individuals accountable for ensuring delivery of what the customer needs and expects; (b) "requirements," or sales funnel activities to be executed; and (c) available resources to accomplish those tasks. For example, when a prospective client is in the "consideration" stage, your organization might share testimonials about your service with him or her. These testimonials could be in digital form (email or video) or physical form (phone conference or meeting).

Not only does a CRM approach that's focused on the customer's purchase journey help shift and keep the spotlight on the customer, but it also clearly defines roles and delivery expectations. What's more, when you bring the customer purchase journey to the top of your process design, you will see enormous synergies emerge between marketing, sales, and service teams.

Perhaps what's most critical in the long term is that you can replicate the system regardless of how your customer or consumer might buy from you, whether it be an in-person sales consultation, a phone call, or a transaction over your website.

Regardless, matching your sales funnel stages to the customer purchase journey may be what's needed to truly revolutionize your customer relationship management initiatives.

Growing Markets—More, New, or Better?

Once you've worked through the customer journey map, we move to activating your growth strategy. Can your brand or business bring more, new, or better value to a given customer segment with your offering? This question can provoke additional thought and drive clarity into your value proposition design. If you fail to position your offering under one of these three descriptors—*more, new,* or *better* value—you'll find it increasingly difficult to stand out or remain relevant in a crowded and competitive marketplace.

As you contemplate market expansion and reaching a new target audience, it's imperative you consider the value proposition map, as well as the "more, new, or better" question. Make these exercises a priority. What follows next could be the design of a statement that will help communicate your value proposition across your stakeholder groups.

Access and activate new markets.

If your organization has pursued (or is in the process of pursing) new growth opportunities, you've most likely identified a new market of growth opportunity for your brand or business. Let me pre-warn you, however: *Identifying* new markets and *accessing* new markets are two vastly different challenges. As you move toward accessing and ultimately, activating a new market or markets, there is a very important capability you need in your arsenal.

My firm was recently hired by a medium-size family business to develop and execute an overall business expansion strategy. After facing external industry challenges, on-going competitive pressures, and growth that had plateaued, they were primed and ready for a change in approach.

> *All great strategies are a result of a big discovery.*

While the resulting growth strategy for this particular client was comprehensive, I want to highlight an important part of the development process we utilized to create an innovative new product development strategy for the organization.

Since this client had garnered enough insights on their target audience through prior strategy work, we elected to move directly into the ideation and business case phase of the strategy. However, I would highly suggest an extensive body of research to understand your target audience *prior* to ideation.

Your organization's ability to innovate—create new products, services and experiences—is critical in building a growth-centered organization. With that said, it's vital that you establish strategy elements first, before you proceed into the development phases.

We subscribe to the notion that all great strategies are a result of a big discovery. In other words, your new product or service development ideas should flow from:

1. a solid understanding of solution gaps that might exist in your markets;

2. unmet needs that lie at the heart of your customer target.

Moving your new discovery to a complete solution, ready-for-market delivery, is not an easy task by any stretch of the imagination. The best way to begin this process is by formulating a strong business case or hypothesis on the products or services you believe your organization should develop as part of a cohesive growth strategy.

To help guide you through this process, I suggest completing a simple business case template. The template provides structure, allowing you to organize your discoveries, and ultimately helps reveal which ideas deserve more research and validation.

The Business Case Template

When business development activates a new market, it is essentially testing and pursuing several "go-to-market" access points or paths simultaneously. Those paths typically are best managed on a tactical roadmap with appropriate metrics over a predetermined period of time. The objective is to narrow or prioritize the different points, based on performance, that business development determines are the most productive path(s) forward to realize the share and revenue targets in the strategy. This is called a business case template (see Figure 2.4).

I highly recommend you keep your business case template confidential or protected, as your ideas might eventually qualify for intellectual property protection.

Across the top of a table, create space for five or six different product or service solutions (only one extra column is shown in Figure 2.4 due to space limitations). You may not utilize that many columns, or you may need to create more. During our work with a large manufacturing client, we discussed nine different products, which were eventually narrowed down to three for the next phase. Think of this table as a formal brainstorming map to organize your innovation possibilities side by side.

Business Case Template (hypothesis document)	
Products/Services	1 (example)
Category	*skin*
Sub-Category	*facial*
Specific Condition or Problem	*aging and excess sun*
Competitive Set (what exists in the category)	*Creams exist but are ineffective, no eraser concepts*
Descriptor for Proposed Product Idea	*sun marks eraser pen*
Target Audience	*50+, primarily female*
Size of Market	*$250 million*
Right To Win (core strengths leveraged)	*retailer relationships*
Right To Win (capabilities needed)	*design, manufacturing, branding*
Rational Consumer Unmet Need or Market Gap That It Solves	*how to get rid of sun marks without excessive surgery*
Emotional Consumer Need Met	*50 is "the new 40"—looking and feeling young*
Go-To-Market/Business Model	*direct sales*
Product, Delivery, or Other	*product and delivery*
Unique Attribute 1	*skin-friendly eraser pad*
Unique Attribute 2	*vibrating pulse on end of pen lifts sun marks from skin*
Unique Attribute 3	*refillable erasers purchased separately*

Figure 2.4: Business Case Template

Once this table is complete, you will proceed to narrow the field to two or three products that will undergo a next round of research and validation before being "development-ready."

Next, identify simple criteria for organizing your business case and list these along the left-hand side of the table. In this case, I am using a fictitious product (for the skin) in column 1 to serve as an example of the kind of information needed at this stage.

With respect to the criteria listed in the left hand column, the top and bottom third grouping of items are fairly self-explanatory at this stage. The section deserving more explanation is the middle third.

In the context of our fictitious example, I've provided some additional color as to the focus in each area:

Target audience: Who is the primary audience for the new product or service? Our hypothesis is that the largest segment of the audience is likely to be female, age fifty or older. While we may reach other age groups, we are concerned most about the largest segment at this stage.

Market size: Having basic information on our target audience as well as the problem(s) our idea solves allows us to get a surface idea of the total market size in potential dollars. We can potentially use that information to evaluate what kind of market share we might expect against the segment of consumers looking for these kinds of solutions. Ultimately, this information will be critical in evaluating which ideas move forward or not.

> *One of the biggest challenges for organizations of all sizes is capturing, aggregating, and acting on customer insights.*

"Right to win" competitive advantage *(core strengths leveraged)*: One of the best ways to grow into new markets, products, or services is to leverage existing strengths you possess as an organization. In this particular example, I cite "retailer relationships." The hypothesis is that we have a portfolio of current products in position with established retail relationships. Those relationships serve as an open door for bringing additional products to market, even if they are outside our core product categories.

"Right to win" competitive advantage *(capabilities needed)*: With new products or services, you're likely to uncover capability gaps in your organization. In this particular area, I identify our belief that we may require design and manufacturing capabilities to bring this new innovation to life, but also to compete and create a long-term position in the space.

Rational need/gap met: What is the specific problem the idea solves for this particular audience? In this case, the fictitious skin product would remove sunspots without the need for surgery. The rational need that it ultimately addresses (to be vetted further in the next stage) would be less expense than cosmetic surgery, less hassle, and greater convenience and ease of diminishing sun spots.

Emotional need/gap met: Based on the points outlined above for rational needs, an emotional need, therefore, would address how the solution makes your target audience feel. In this case, the emotional needs tend to be along the lines of "feeling young," "healthy," or "ageless."

Go-to-market/business model: Lastly, you might use this item to identify an early hypothesis describing how to best get your new product or service to your target audience or market. In this case, I chose to identify direct sales as a viable path to market for this new skin product. Another option might be to license the skin product to a large manufacturer to distribute under a recognizable consumer brand. Or perhaps we decide that B2B sales to dermatologists and physician offices is the best fit. Maybe it's appropriate to explore a subscription model through e-commerce to distribute the refillable erasers for our skin pen.

The example provided in column 1 should give you a feel for the detail needed to complete the business case template. While your information does not need absolute accuracy or feasibility yet, you should have enough baseline knowledge to serve as a hypothesis.

It's the "Start" That Stops Most Businesses

As you develop your business case template, keep in mind the insights for product or service expansion often already exist within your organization, your people, and the unique desires of your customers. Without question, one of the biggest challenges for organizations of all sizes is capturing, aggregating, and acting on customer insights.

> *There is nothing safe about innovation and growth. And, conversely, there is nothing safe about doing nothing.*

In other words, it's the start that stops most businesses, isn't it? The front-end ambiguity and perceived risk associated with innovation sends most of us back to comfortable hiding areas in the business.

There is nothing safe about

innovation and growth. And, conversely, there is nothing safe about doing nothing, is there? So ... what risk would you rather take?

Having the mettle to act on customer insights is ultimately what will distance you from the pack. The business case template is designed to be the starting point for you to put movement behind your insights and ideas.

Choosing the Right Growth Strategy for Your Business

Sometimes choices seem so easy, right? It doesn't matter which donut you pick—chocolate, old fashioned, sugar, or filled—any donut will be wonderful and satisfying.

But when it comes to choosing the right growth strategy for your business, it can be very easy to make the *wrong* choice.

Which path is the right one for your business?

The choice you make should be highly informed by insight-led research pertaining to your customers, the marketplace, external changes, and trends. The choice you make will define where and how you will grow your business in the immediate future. If only it were as easy as picking a donut from the display case! But this choice will require precise direction to those you lead regarding what to do next.

Roadmap for Growth: Four Options

Consider this high-level roadmap for choosing your growth strategy. Assuming you have spent adequate time in the research phase and have uncovered where the opportunities lie for your brands and/or organization, there are essentially four options for growth.

As outlined below, 'products' is meant to refer to the products and services you sell, and 'markets' generally refers to the target audience to whom you sell your products and services. Markets can comprise channels of trade or geography, as an example.

1. Current Products to Current Markets

Of the four growth choices, this particular path focuses on building your market share to *a known audience* with *known products*. This strategy may require extra thought regarding how to sell the same product or service across different channels while controlling critical attributes such as assortment, price and experience. A familiar example is Apple. In its earliest days, Apple gradually expanded the distribution of their devices across multiple outlets, including the likes of Walmart and Target. The overall Apple assortment and experience can be reduced or increased depending on the target audience in that respective channel.

John Deere is another brand that executes well on delivering a more sophisticated assortment of products in channels where expertise and service is highest, while bringing more basic products to retailers such as Home Depot where the target audience is accustomed to making buying decisions without assistance.

2. Current Products to New Markets

In this particular strategy, you choose to take your *current products* to *new, adjacent markets* where you don't currently compete. The hurdles you face may possibly include tweaking your product to meet specifications with your new target audience or finding expertise in personnel for a new market. However, the reward can be substantial—access to an entirely new market space.

A terrific example of current products to new markets is the Google lineup of Chromebooks, designed to be a lightweight, lower-price-point, cloud-based laptop. Chromebooks have done extremely well in consumer markets, and Google has expanded the product into educational markets, where it's adding tremendous value in schools for enhanced learning.

3. New Products to Current Markets

Making the choice to develop *new products*, whether launching into *current* or *existing* markets, is not one to be made lightly. Product development exercises new organizational muscles—and taking on too much, too fast can result in injury. However, new insights can lead to tremendous opportunity for your brand, not to mention incremental sales growth in new categories or new price points. Typically, new products are launched to the same target market or audience to cater to an unmet need or new discovery.

Another familiar example, illustrative of new products to current markets, would be Keurig's new Rivo, designed for cappuccino and espresso lovers. Rivo broadens the Keurig line beyond the k-cup coffee brewers and furthers their penetration into consumer markets.

4. New Products to New Markets

Developing *new products* and then launching them in *unfamiliar (new) markets* is one of the more difficult paths of the four, but certainly has the chance to be quite rewarding. The new product development will need to take into account different tastes, preferences, and requirements in terms of your new target audience. This doesn't even begin to address the capabilities you need to get your final product in the hands of the end user, whether it be supply chain or distribution related. Restaurants wishing to expand to new geography (countries) are often forced to create new products and or adjust ingredients in an effort to cater to a new audience.

Once you choose one of the four growth options, you and your team need to define how the business will execute the strategy. This will most likely require an extensive audit of your current capabilities, as well as identifying the new capabilities you will need. You might then decide to acquire the capabilities, build them, or outsource them.

> *Your strategic plan should be the instruction manual for your overall strategy.*

So, of the four different paths, which one is most relevant to your business?

Strategy Questions That Need Answers

As you make choices about your go-forward strategy (based on an increased understanding of your organizational identity and customer experience), you'll be taking calculated risks, as well as developing new initiatives. Let's turn now to several key questions and considerations to guide you as you develop your business growth initiatives for the coming year.

In chapter 3, I will outline some of the common mistakes we make as leaders when it comes to growth strategy (see "Why Your Strategy Isn't Working"). One critical area of focus is the tendency leaders have to blend or re-order the strategic planning process with the business strategy. The important distinction is that your strategic plan should be the instruction manual for your overall strategy.

> *You need to be simultaneously serving markets and building new ones—this is at the heart of strategy.*

If you've ever used a navigational mapping program on your smartphone, tablet, or desktop before, then you've probably used the zooming tools to see where you're going, where you've been, or if there are alternative routes to your destination.

While many of us are most concerned with the "next turn" or the traffic patterns on our current route, it's time to zoom out. If growth is your priority, you need to be simultaneously serving markets *and* building new ones—this is at the heart of strategy. So, how do you know which markets to build for your business? These three words are your zooming tools: *learning, insight,* and *discovery.*

What new learning did you capture this year?

Let's look at the first zooming tool: learning. The learning organization is a growing organization. Very specifically, what new learning did you capture this past year? These learnings might originate in the form of market research, industry trends, competitive intelligence, target audience focus groups, or discoveries you've made through better data analytics in your business. Learning insights can be as simple as garnering deeper understanding of your end-user's unfulfilled needs as they relate your product or service.

What new possibilities exist?

Asking your organization, "What new possibilities exist?" can yield powerful discoveries. These new insights should illuminate possibilities for your products or services to serve a new segment of customers, a new demographic of customers or perhaps customers in a new geography. It's these very specific discoveries that drive growth and unearth markets in which your products and services may be—or currently are—underserved.

What new growth initiatives will you pursue?

Let's look at the third zoom tool, which is discovery. Now that you've discovered possible markets for new growth, next on the agenda is establishing some priority areas for growth in for the upcoming year. In other words, which new markets will you pursue? In some organizations,

> *The "how" starts with "who."*

the discovery process can lead to a long wish list of "shiny" opportunities. While they may all have some merit, further analysis should help you prioritize the growth initiatives against the investment you wish to allocate for each.

Of course, recalling the concepts we've already explored in this chapter, including adding value to the customer experience and connecting products to markets, here are five additional filters that might help you determine which initiatives to pursue:

- What is the size of the market you wish to reach?
- How relevant are your core competencies in that particular market?
- How important is this particular customer segment or market to your business now and in the long-term?
- Can you bring more, new or better value to this new customer segment with your offering?
- What, if any, new capabilities will you need to build to reach a particular market?

Who will lead your growth initiatives?

Finally, perhaps most critical at this point are the beginning discussions regarding *who*, from a leadership standpoint, will be accountable for driving a particular growth initiative forward. Deciding on the area you would like to grow the business is the first step. *How* you will do it is the next important decision. The "how" starts with "who." Specifically, you need to define your ideal "who" first and then look to the current organization to evaluate a possible fit—not the reverse. You may need to find different talent for specific growth initiatives. When well-defined and research-backed growth initiatives sputter, look first at how (and, in what order) you addressed the "who" part of the puzzle.

> *When well-defined and research-backed growth initiatives sputter, look first at how (and, in what order) you addressed the "who" part of the puzzle.*

Getting the right leadership in place behind your most important growth initiatives is how you demonstrate commitment to a growth initiative. It then becomes that leader's role to put the right structure, talent and tactical plan in place to bring the plan to life.

Don't miss this opportunity to zoom-out on your business and get the growth strategy right. In addition to identifying and prioritizing new markets for growth, you'll find the exploration process especially insightful as you continue to grow in your existing markets—not to mention the value in exploring your talent needs at a strategic and leadership level that's consistent with your planned-for growth.

So, while we have spent a lot of time on the "how" in this section, stay tuned as we begin to explore the "who" as it relates to your growth strategy.

The Secret Growth Strategy of the Ant Colony

What's your next move?

If you've ever lived in the southeast region of the country, then you've also more than likely hired a monthly pesticide service.

After moving to Georgia six years ago, my wife and I quickly dismissed our realtor's strong recommendation to hire a pest control service. "We don't need a pest control service—we'll be fine!" I thought.

Even after seeing multiple pest control trucks parked in driveways throughout the neighborhood, we remained convinced that we did not need another monthly bill. Besides, with the way we clean house, we believed there was no possible way any bugs could have an interest in our house.

After a few weeks, we were quickly introduced to Georgia's diverse, large, and growing population of pests who made it their mission to infiltrate our home. They succeeded.

Each spring brings droves and droves of ants to our home—and not just the kind that march in a line looking for crumbs but move along on their mission minding their own business. No, these ants swarm and sting. They establish a nest and slowly take over the space they invade. Since moving to Georgia, we have seen our new friend, the pest control expert, quite frequently.

Upon our specialist's last visit, he explained how the ants work. While there may be thousands of ants back at the nest, only one or two ants are sent out of the colony to scout for food or "ant-treasure." Upon discovery, the lone ant reports back to the nest to which thousands of ants are then deployed in pursuit of the new treasure.

> *Every business needs someone who travels ahead to discover new trends, markets, or opportunities.*

Our most recent ant invasion got me thinking more about the "who" of growth strategy and initiatives.

The Chief Growth Officer

Every business has accountants and attorneys who help the business remain accurate and legal. Most business people would not dare attempt to conduct these tasks on their own without this valuable expertise, especially for complex businesses that need to adhere to intricate regulations. In the same way, no one would try to perform surgery on their own knee when there is a specialist who is trained to repair knee injuries.

Why then would a business allow generalists to handle complex growth projects—generalists who only know what is and has been?

> *Does your organization have a scout? Do you have someone accountable for driving a cohesive approach to strategy and growth for your organization?*

A new destination and a new journey are what most companies are seeking right now, and this fact is giving rise to a new kind of professional: a growth specialist.

Like the ant population, every organization, team, executive, and CEO needs a scout.

Every business needs someone who travels ahead to discover new trends, markets, or opportunities. Organizations need someone with single accountability for the future growth of the business, unencumbered by political lines, territories or self-promotion.

The current approach to business strategy typically tasks functional leaders with figuring out where and how the organization will grow. While this has served well in the past, the current fast-moving external environment coupled with unstable economic conditions and rapid entrepreneurial disruption demands a new approach.

Does your organization have a scout?

Dale Buss, author at *Chief Executive* magazine, penned a terrific article entitled "Chief Growth Officer." This job title has caught fire in many innovative organizations.[9] The thrust of Buss's case is that business leaders need to find a way to keep growth at the forefront of the organization and ultimately, from slipping into the shadows of the day-to-day priorities.

When it comes time to decide how and where your business will grow, you need a person at your side who will not only challenge your current thinking and stretch your capabilities, but also be a guide for you and your organization on the journey to new growth. A growth specialist is not just a visionary, but a navigator as well.

This new kind of professional is different—much different. They are the ones blazing the trail in front of you. And that is the only way to make certain you will land on the road less traveled—the road to lasting, healthy growth and success.

Unfortunately, not every business will hire a Chief Growth Officer (CGO) to help access the next big market for growth. If not a CGO, then I suggest partnering with the expert outsider is the secret sauce to establishing the right "scout-to-nest" cross-functional relationship—needed not just to *access* the right opportunities, but to *activate* them.

> *Power is shifting to consumers and customers, forcing brands to ensure that virtually every aspect of future strategies are customer-centric.*

I love what growth strategist Andy Birol said in *Upstart Business Journal*: "Business ownership has so little accountability and oversight that without devil's advocates and contrarian data/insight to strike a balance, dysfunction is likely."[10] The advisory relationship is paramount for you and your staff.

Does your organization have a scout? Do you have somebody accountable for driving a cohesive approach to strategy and growth for your organization? If not, now may be the time to change your approach.

So, Mr. or Ms. CEO or Business Owner—*go get a scout!*

How to Get Your Business Ready for the Next-Generation Consumer

Vital strategic changes don't end with designation of a Chief Growth Officer, however. Appointing a CGO is only one step, albeit a crucial one, in preparing for a major whirlwind about to hit the business landscape: the next-generation consumer. Preparing for the customer of the future is a bit (or a lot) like preparing for a natural disaster.

Being prepared for an earthquake or tornado is extremely difficult given how fast they strike, with little to no warning at all. Essentially, you are given a few minutes to grab your family and flee to an area of cover—and pray and hope for the best. Coupling the suddenness factor with the sheer power of these events, the outcome is particularly challenging to predict.

Hurricanes are much different. The majority of hurricanes are predicted days or weeks in advance as they take shape and form over oceans thousands of miles from land. Weather experts and computer models predict possible paths, wind strength and the like. While difficult to achieve pinpoint accuracy, the population is given enough warning to prepare for the incoming storm—whether by boarding up windows and doors, or sand bagging rivers and streams.

If you're part of the business "population" (whether providing services, products, or both) you may already be aware of a predicted hurricane on the horizon. Already forming and taking shape, the "Hurricane Consumer" will be here in 2020 and beyond, and that consumer will be bigger and more powerful than you can imagine. While some businesses have made preparations already, there are certainly many dragging behind. But, there is time still to prepare.

In an article entitled "20 Quotes on How Your Business Must Change by 2020," John Brandon presents a collection of expert insights across such topics as augmented reality, mobility, transparency in culture, rapid learning, and millennials.[11] Without question, the common thread headline is that power is shifting to consumers and customers, forcing brands to ensure that virtually every aspect of future strategies are customer-centric.

Among several other quotations from the article, Brian Solis offers the following insight: "Businesses that place people and what they feel, think, do and share as a priority in not just product design but overall marketing and business strategy outperform those who don't. It's about a journey that knows no end—only how to keep the passengers delighted and valued."

Along similar lines, Augie Ray adds that in the future, organizations will need to leverage social media (among other channels) to deliver a better customer experience. And further, Sebastian Kemmler adds that retail store design should be optimized to produce "shareable content" so much so that retailers begin measuring posts per square foot/meter, not just revenue per square foot/meter. Ray's and Kemmler's comments lift the strategic importance of social media in how organizations will be required to shape better customer and employee relationships.

And, if you need more proof that social media is worth your precious time and investment, according to the Content Marketing Institute, 78 percent of Americans say social media impacts their purchasing decisions. What's more, 74 percent of marketers saw an increase in consumer traffic from spending just six hours on social media. Organizations will need to see social media as more than the latest fad or simply part of a checklist of daily tasks if they want to compete and survive through 2020 and beyond. Additionally, I argue organizations need to see content creation and curation as a pillar in their digital strategy if they want further separation from competing brands.

Thus, the big challenge is how to be sure your business is prepared for this hurricane. To help you focus your efforts, I've organized a preliminary "hurricane-readiness kit" consisting of two central themes with the critical topics needed to move your teams into action:

Digitalization of Everything

It's time to integrate the physical and digital world.

If you don't already have a team member on your board of directors or advisory board with expertise in the digital space, you should. If you don't have a board, perhaps this is a position on your executive team. The bottom line is that you need high-level commitment via expertise and experience to move digital into a priority seat for your organization now. Are you digital?

From homes to cars and everything in between, more of the products you use in our everyday life will be "connected." You need a cross-functional task force charged with looking closely at how to make your products and services "smart," allowing more habit-forming engagement for your customers or consumers. If everything people do in the future comes at the touch or swipe of a finger, you need to be there, too, or risk being left out in the cold. What parts of your business are "smart"? Could that be an opportunity for new engagement?

Put your brand at their fingertips.

Personalization of Everything

Delight your customers with a personalized experience!

Every single person in the organization needs to be an extension of customer service, including sales, marketing, operations, and finance. *Everybody* exists to personalize the customer experience. Personalization can show up in the form of products that can be individualized to consumer tastes, cer-

> **Everybody in the organization exists to personalize the customer experience.**

tain preferences in shipping methods, and interactions on social media—all a result of knowing the customer better. *How well do you know your customer?*

Developing a more individualized experience for your consumers may represent opportunity number one. And it starts with knowing your customer better than your competition does so you can tweak, shape and form the entire end-to-end experience with your organization. As we discussed earlier in this chapter, you need a cross-functional task force charged with developing a thorough purchasing journey map to leverage the ultimate customer

> *Design everything to delight!*

experience, from the design of your products to how they are marketed, purchased, and shared. Design everything to delight!

Seriously consider a content creation strategy if you haven't already. Under personalization of everything, your current customers are your brand, so include them in your content creation. Are you designed to delight?

Perhaps this is your warning bell to begin making changes in your organization. By the next generation, the consumer will have very different expectations of brands, from how we design products and services to how we deliver the complete experience.

Get to know your customer or consumer inside and out, as by the time the next decade rolls around, your entire organization will be designed to delight beyond anything anyone has ever seen before.

A hurricane is coming. Are you prepared?

Three Ways Portfolio Thinking Transforms Business Strategy

Along with digitization and personalization, portfolio thinking is another strategic business concept that cannot be ignored. But what does it mean?

The word 'portfolio' can conjure up thoughts of your personal investment portfolio or even the person entrusted to oversee your personal assets.

The entire first page of Google search results involving the phrase 'portfolio management' delivers items pertaining to investment services or the "art or science of matching investment choices to specific objectives" within one's investment portfolio.

The word 'portfolio' can also refer to a collection of achievements, artwork, or other creations of significant value to a person. You might display a portfolio or share it with others to demonstrate your capabilities or track record in an effort to build trust and confidence.

In total, the word 'portfolio' is highly personal and engaging, isn't it?

From making the right investment choices to building a collection of accomplishments, a portfolio represents a valuable asset that you're motivated to protect and enhance. Naturally, something that's emotional or engaging drives focus, energy, and extensive thought.

So again, what on earth is portfolio thinking, and what does it have to do with growing your business?

Portfolio thinking pulls the market in.

Typically, there are two approaches organizations utilize in building a growth strategy. In starting with a growth objective, a strategic planning effort might take on an internal-based, top-down approach that sees opportunity through the current business, brands, products or services. Conversely, an external-based strategic approach sees opportunity from the marketplace back into the business. Which one most describes your business?

There may be times in the business life cycle when one approach trumps another, but largely, creating a long-term growth strategy will demand an externally based approach.

Portfolio thinking asks, "What else should or could we be doing to enhance or expand the business?" Portfolio thinking encourages us to go wide before getting narrow, triggering curiosity and research. It asks, "What are we missing?" and orients the entire strategy process to the outside first.

Portfolio thinking organizes opportunity.

Similar to making personal investment choices, portfolio thinking is the art and science of identifying, selecting, organizing and managing growth opportunities. An externally-based focus uncovers possible insights and growth opportunities that present a unique fit to a specific competency you might possess, an audience you currently serve, or perhaps a new market expansion initiative.

A portfolio strategy is not only a roadmap for achieving your growth targets, but it becomes a foundation for how you organize and manage each opportunity within the organization.

Let's consider a manufacturing business in the lawn and garden space. The business might choose to organize a portfolio of market expansion opportunities by growth forecasted, geography, channel, or perhaps, trend. Therefore, a portfolio based on growth forecasted or trend in lawn and garden care might organize across the following three buckets: self-propelled equipment, "connected" equipment (i.e., IoT, or Internet of Things) and robotics.

While maintaining a leadership position in a more mature space such as self-propelled equipment is important, beginning to build businesses that intersect with future, high growth markets is critical. In this example, portfolio thinking should help management structure these opportunities according to their respective life cycle stage. In this example, one market is mature while the other market is in development.

> *Portfolio thinking creates a sense of ownership.*

By organizing the business growth strategy into a portfolio, you can make smart choices regarding both *where* and *how* to allocate time, money, and resources.

Portfolio thinking creates ownership.

Perhaps most intriguing, portfolio thinking creates a sense of ownership. As the owner of a portfolio, you're heavily invested in caring for that portfolio's performance. Within an organization, you might designate or organize talent around a specific pillar within your portfolio of growth opportunities. Simplistically, you might choose to align more seasoned talent to a core pillar (existing products, existing markets) in the portfolio, while selecting specialized or expert talent to non-core (new products, new markets) pillars in the portfolio.

So, let me ask you: Could portfolio thinking be a missing link in your business strategy? If implemented, how could portfolio thinking impact your execution of strategy?

Portfolio thinking pulls the outside in, organizes growth, and drives ownership. Could it be you need that kind of thinking to break through tough growth challenges? For this reason, portfolio thinking is one of several key strategic elements to drive growth, which I'll review in the next section.

Six Strategic Shifts to Drive Growth

Do you find yourself frustrated trying to uncover what went wrong with last year's growth strategy? Has a recent acquisition failed to deliver the growth you expected? Perhaps you're getting ready to make another investment and you want to be sure you position the company to capitalize on growth opportunity.

It's these questions that litter conference room whiteboards with discussion and debate as companies of all sizes plan for the year ahead. If this describes your organization, you're not alone.

The following strategic shifts, most of which we've already explored in this chapter, warrant serious consideration in your team and organization:

1. Growing and Serving Employees First

Are you growing the people in your organization?

While you're focused on growing the numbers, don't forget to grow your people.

As we have discussed in this chapter, there is a two-fold employee development strategy that will enhance your ability to keep and magnetize customers. First, you must know your target customers deeply enough to learn what kind of employee talent you need in key roles in order to provide the consistent level of service you desire. Second, you need to serve your employees *first*.

Our family business had over 350 employees.

If you do not treat your employee family as if they are your customers, they will never know how to treat their customers, in turn. Customers transformed by your service or product actively seek to be magnetized— meaning they want multiple reasons to advocate for you. One of those reasons is not that your employees provide service, but rather the *manner* in which your employees actually serve them.

Do you have a development plan for each employee that will challenge him or her to grow professionally and personally? Are your leaders held accountable for developing more leaders, and/or providing the right coaching approach to grow your employees? If you're successful in growing your employees, they will be successful in growing your customers.

2. Moving the Spotlight *from* the Competition *to* the Customer

Focus your spotlight on the customer!

Most teams and businesses find revenue building to be the ultimate uphill climb. They almost always struggle as a pack on the hill, side-by-side, trying to power forward against what seems to be a Tour de France-like incline, fighting heavy headwinds.

While the uphill climb to generate leads and acquire new customers certainly makes the list of priorities, there may be another path to the top of the hill—possibly a path with much less resistance.

Customer loyalty is magnetic

What is this path? *The customers you already have.*

If done correctly, developing strategies to better serve your *current* customers not only builds attachment to your brand, but it also builds a magnet for your brand. I love the imagery of a customer as a magnet for you and your

> *You need to earn your customers' loyalty and advocacy by delivering a memorable experience.*

brand—going beyond loyalty to *advocacy*. As you transform your customers with your product or service, you magnetize them to attract more of your ideal audience to your brand or movement.

This strategy goes hand in hand with understanding the customer experience. In an age where the likes of Starbucks, Zappos, Amazon, and the Apple Store continue to amaze and impress with exceptional customer experiences, the bar for the rest

> *75 percent of Americans are likely to speak positively about a company after a good customer service experience, contrasting 59 percent who are likely to speak negatively about a company after poor service.*

of us. You need to earn your customers' loyalty and advocacy by delivering a memorable experience. As we discussed, one of the best ways to accomplish this is to better understand your customers' purchasing journey (see Figure 2.3: The Customer Journey Map).

Where do your customers start? Where do they get stuck? What requirements must be met before they commit or purchase? If you've never mapped your customers' journey to purchase, now is the time. Innovation in experience should be one of your top five growth initiatives. According to American Express, 75 percent of Americans are likely to speak positively about a company after a good customer service experience, contrasting 59 percent who are likely to speak negatively about a company after poor service.

Don't put this one off or your brand will easily slip into irrelevance with the ever-discerning American consumer.

3. Sharpening Your Value Proposition

There are gaps in the marketplace, as defined by your customers, and your charge is to uncover them and design a proposition that plugs the hole. The value you add is an intersection and the world wants to meet you there. The intersection is where your unique strengths collide with the unique needs of those you serve.

- What unique strengths does your organization possess that meet the unique needs of those you serve?
- Are your strengths divergent from your competition?

Describe how the value you add will impact your customers when done right. Describe how the customers will feel and act,

> *Too often, our energies become easily consumed in beating the competition instead of building value for the customer.*

how your goods or services might change them for the better and how you envision them sharing their experience with your product or service.

Added value—where your strengths intersect customer needs.

Too often, our energies become easily consumed in *beating* the competition instead of *building value* for the customer. In order to deliver real long-term value, challenge your team to go deep in understanding your customer segments, unmet needs and areas for delivering a better experience with your product or service. This shift in mindset leads to new insights in both your market space and your customer segments and will ultimately illuminate incredible potential for new value.

4. Moving Customers to Advocate for You

Moving customers *from* loyalty *to* advocacy is perhaps the holy grail of any business, but, as mentioned, it happens to be one of the largest gaps existing in organizations of all sizes. While marketing and sales departments are focused on creating repeat purchasers, very few have really mastered moving customers to a stage where they actively share your brand with others. Obviously, one popular way to do this is through social media vehicles where it's easy for your customers to share your brand with their friends.

A big consideration in your advocacy strategy should include community building, whether through your website, events, advisory initiatives, or other platforms, with the goal of bringing like-minded and like-hearted customers together.

It's through a community strategy that customers can hone, refine and share their stories both electronically and in-person. A perfect example of this is the EggFest program developed by The Big Green Egg Grill. EggFest is designed to bring Big Green Egg grilling fanatics together in local markets. Consumers learn more about cooking with their Green Egg from brand experts, as well as other loyal customers, not to mention being infused with the brand story (the reason *why* they purchased their Big Green Egg in the first place). Armed with new recipes, new friends, and new ideas, these loyal customers then return home to share their love of the brand with others.

> *Growth-centered organizations build people, customers, and value.*

It's called being magnetized. Growth-centered organizations build people, customers, and value.

If one of more of these strategies is on your radar now, you're on your way to building an endless flow of new customers.

Customers are waiting to be transformed into magnets for your brand … so what are you waiting for?

5. Strategic Innovation

Effective content marketing needs to be part of your strategic plan.

Lack of innovation, if not addressed, can have a significant impact on the long-term health of your business, leading to painful and debilitating periods of customer defect and flat-to-no sales growth. If you want to matter to your customer now and in the future, you need to be bringing insight-led products, services, and experiences to market.

One important strategic innovation along these lines is effective content marketing. If content marketing is not on your agenda, it needs to be. As highlighted in this chapter, whether you serve businesses or consumers, building a digital relationship with your end customer is a powerful driver of loyalty and advocacy.

So, what kind of content should you begin to produce? It depends on your brand promise. How do you seek to transform customers through your products or services? If you're in the business of home furnishings, you're helping to enhance your customers' homes and subsequently, their lives. You could, as an example, provide on-going inspiration or advice on important home decor trends, techniques and products. As you become a valued and trusted expert in your specific domain, you foster attachment to your own brand and business.

Think in terms of how you might build an extended, always-on, connectedness with your customers so that you become an indispensable resource—whether it be through your physical location(s) or your digital location. A presence across multiple medias makes it easier for customers to access and, ultimately, to share your brand.

6. Strategic Investment

Finally, let's revisit the importance of effective portfolio thinking. Companies that market several brands or services can easily fall in the trap of being wide and shallow. In the back half of 2014, we saw the likes of GE, Procter & Gamble, and IBM sell non-core brands or businesses to allow a re-focus on fewer, bigger, faster growing segments. Even in smaller organizations, it's common to see product development and marketing budget dollars spread evenly across brands. Based on research and analysis, companies should be placing bets on fewer areas for growth where they can shift investment.

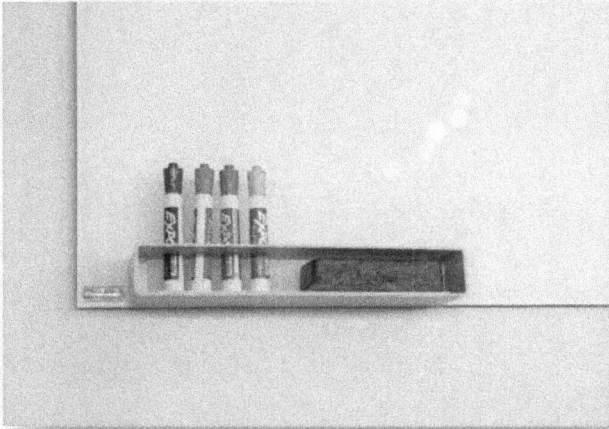

Customers who have been magnetized to your quest feel as if your services and products were made just for them. Investing in and developing your employees will result in a workforce that is driven to create value for your customers. As your organization builds value, you build customers who become loyal and eventually, magnetized. And you build value through innovative initiatives and investments.

The opportunity is now. You and your team can emerge from the conference room whiteboard session victoriously with a clear picture of what strategic growth shifts need to occur. Which of the six shifts mentioned above has the potential to release new growth for your organization in the coming year?

WORKBOOK

Chapter 2 Questions

Question: Who are you as an organization, and whom do you serve? Where is your current strategy focused? How can your strategy focus more effectively on the customer? How can it focus more effectively on adding value?

_____

_____

_____

_____

_____

_____

_____

_____

_____

_____

_____

_____

Question: What growth stage is your business at, and where do you want it to go next? What are some specific ways you will get there?

_____

_____

_____

_____

_____

_____

_____

_____

_____

_____

_____

Question: How do you envision your business and brand changing your industry?

_____

_____

_____

_____

_____

_____

_____

_____

_____

_____

_____

Question: What are your organization's strengths? What are your customers' needs? What makes you stand apart?

_____

_____

_____

_____

_____

_____

_____

_____

_____

_____

_____

Question: What are the components of your customers' purchase journey (see Figure 2.3)? Where can you improve?

_____

_____

_____

_____

_____

_____

_____

_____

_____

_____

Question: What new markets should you be aiming for? How can you access and activate them?

_____

_____

_____

_____

_____

_____

_____

_____

_____

_____

_____

Question: What is your strategy for connecting current products to current markets? Current products to new markets? New products to current markets? New products to new markets?

_____

_____

_____

_____

_____

_____

_____

_____

_____

_____

Question: What has your business learned in the past year? What new possibilities exist, and what initiatives might you pursue to act on those possibilities?

_____

_____

_____

_____

_____

_____

_____

_____

_____

_____

_____

Question: Who is your Chief Growth Officer? How do you envision this role within your specific business structure?

_____

_____

_____

_____

_____

_____

_____

_____

_____

Question: Is portfolio-oriented thinking part of your business growth strategy? If so, what does your business's portfolio encompass? If not, how can you adjust or redesign your strategy to include portfolio thinking?

_____

_____

_____

_____

_____

_____

_____

_____

_____

_____

_____

Question: How do you put employees first? How can you grow in this area?

_____

_____

_____

_____

_____

_____

_____

_____

Circle Back: If you haven't done so already, create an intentional business growth strategy, and focus it primarily on the customer and on value added—on people and innovation—not on competition. Begin with developing your value proposition. Focus on what makes you stand apart, with a mind to your strengths and how they intersect with your customers' needs.

Assess where your business is currently and where you want to go. Plot a roadmap to connect current and new products to current and new markets. As you explore how to access and activate new markets, continue to serve your employees, as well as your customers, in order to lay a foundation for healthy, sustainable growth. Understand your customers and their purchase journey so you can win them over as advocates for your brand.

Make sure your strategy ultimately addresses not only who you are and whom you serve but also what you've learned, where the possibilities are, and how you will act on those possibilities. Organize and take ownership of opportunity with portfolio-oriented thinking. Perhaps most crucially, identify a Chief Growth Officer who can specialize in meeting these and other growth challenges. And in all of these measures, work to create and then realize a vision of your organization and its brand that is so spectacular it will change your industry.

CHAPTER THREE

Grow for It:
Executing Growth-Driven Strategy

People. Process. Results.

These are the three most basic elements in business thinking. And in this chapter, we'll hone in on one powerful formula that will streamline your thinking as you put your business strategy into practice.

One Formula That Changes Everything

While strategy design is vital to an organization's growth, what is even more important is what is *done* with the design.

According to *Dictionary.com,* the word 'executive' is derived from a mid-fifteenth-century term meaning "performed or carried out." Thus, quite simply, the role of the executive is to execute—to ensure jobs are completed.[12]

The question most leaders wrestle with is *how*:

- How can I drive my organization—with more confidence—to achieve the kind of results I desire?
- How can I close the gap that exists between what I say I'm going to do (in my strategy), and what actually gets done (in execution)?
- How can I make sure we start delivering in a repeatable, consistent, and predictable fashion?

I am willing to wager that poor execution is at the root of most, if not all, of your headaches, anxieties, and sleepless nights with respect to your current job performance—and perhaps even your long-term career aspirations.

As I've trained, coached, and led organizations of all sizes and industries, I've come to rely on a simple, back-to-the-basics business formula to evaluate underperformance in execution: *Same* People + *Same* Process = *Same* Results.

> ***Same* People +
> *Same* Process =
> *Same* Results.**

In more cases than not, organizations unhappy with their results eventually find themselves taking a hard look at their people and the processes they use to drive the business. Ultimately, what follows is change.

The goal is always the same: Remove *same* from the equation.

Traits of Successful Executive Teams

While strategy design is vital to an organization's growth, what matters even more is what you *do* with the strategy binder. When it's time to bring the strategy binder to life, does your organization sizzle, or does it fizzle as most do?

Do you know what play is next? Are you flexible enough to react to new opportunity and quick to respond to competitors?

Just as football head coaches and offensive coordinators have the play sheet in-hand during the game, executives need a play sheet to drive their strategy forward in the marketplace. And they need a team to do it—note that the first variable in the business formula with which we opened the chapter is *people*.

> *When it's time to bring the strategy binder to life, does your organization sizzle or fizzle?*

According to an organizational poll I conducted in late 2014, overwhelmingly, the challenge that keeps leaders up at night is executing their strategy in order to deliver the expected results. Since leaders are also balancing demands at home with demands at work, a strong team is important. With this in mind, let's consider several traits successful executive teams have in common—traits that have the power to move people,

> *Great executive teams keep score.*

cultures, and organizations to the highest levels of performance.

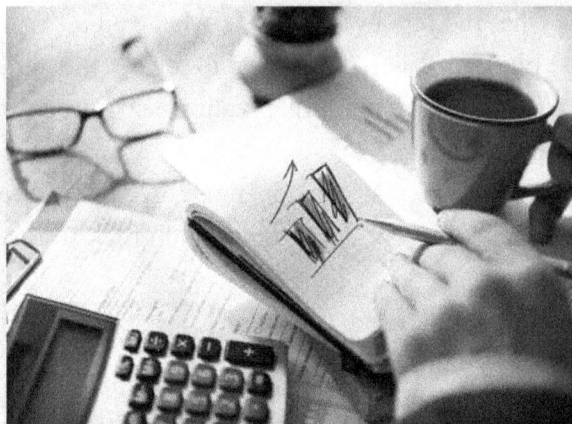

Are you keeping score?

Clarity

Great executive teams keep score. Clarity is as simple as being able to clearly define for the organization the expected outcomes, as well as the tactics, actions or behaviors needed to carry out the strategy. It's not nearly enough to identify revenue and profit outcomes without *linking* the tactics and behaviors required to achieve them.

Once identified, these tactics and behaviors must be clearly defined in the form of key metrics, as well as accessible and/or visible using a scorecard stating organizational and team outcomes. What makes clarity so difficult is identifying the critical metrics that not only drive the right outcomes, but matter the most to the value you promise to deliver to your customers.

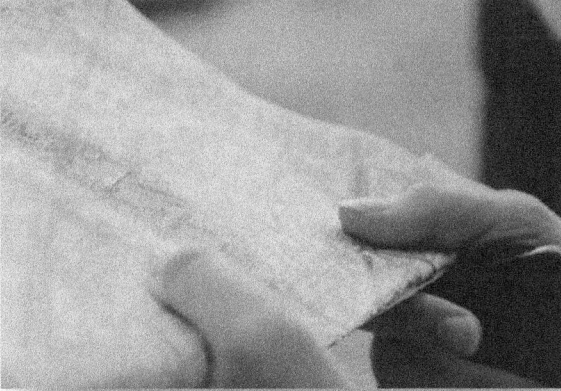

Execution is where the rubber meets the road.

Responsibility

Great executive teams assign ownership. Responsibility is each team member *owning* specific sections or components of the strategy and then actually delivering results. Accordingly, responsibility should cascade through the organization from top to bottom, ensuring every team member

> *Great executive teams assign ownership. They not only hold people to stated commitments, but they also help people reach for their commitments.*

understands how his or her job is linked to the larger organizational strategy and goals.

Do you have a system in place that answers these questions: Who are you responsible for? What are you responsible for delivering? When are you responsible for delivering it?

Honesty and accountability go hand in hand.

Accountability

Great executive teams not only hold people to stated commitments, but they also help people reach for their commitments. First and foremost, every member of the executive leadership team should hold himself or herself to

> *Great executive teams promote honesty, accountability, and high levels of transparency and trust.*

a standard of honesty and accountability in delivering on his or her commitments. And of course, leadership must make the tough and fast decisions necessary to ensure the organization has the right people in the right positions.

However, I propose that executive teams take accountability even further. We all have blind spots or skill gaps that, if not watched carefully, can become detrimental in our ability to execute. I highly encourage leaders to team with cross-functional accountability partners who will keep an eye on potential blind spot tendencies. Accountability partners keep you honest and are another source in ensuring you deliver on your promises.

Transparency and vulnerability cement trust in organizations.

Transparency, Trust, and Vulnerability

Vulnerability is another key ingredient of effective executive teams. It plays a critical role in unlocking deeper levels of transparency and trust, which are hallmarks of growth-oriented teams. When leaders are willing to address topics typically swept under the rug, a deeper team connection develops. Trust levels throughout the organization grow.

> *Leadership's commitment to transparency and willingness to show vulnerability are the components that, ultimately, establish a cement-like trust across the organization.*

Leadership's commitment to transparency and the willingness to show vulnerability are the components that, ultimately, establish a cement-like trust across the organization. Within teams, this kind of culture promotes executives focused on building people who build businesses.

It all starts with you. Strategy ultimately depends on execution, for which you, as a leader, are responsible, especially if you're the chief executive.

In chapter 4, we will revisit vulnerability as a key element of growth-oriented leadership. For now, let's end this section by considering the following two questions:

- In looking at your executive team, which of these leadership traits is missing from your collective repertoire?

- Could this be the missing link in your ability to execute flawlessly on your strategy and unlock dormant growth potential?

Why Your Strategy Isn't Working

In the world of business management research, it has become a commonplace that as many as 90 percent of organizations fail to implement their strategies successfully.[13] Moreover, a collaboration of researchers from Marakon Associates and the Economist Intelligence Unit have found that organizations realize only 60 percent of the potential value of their strategies.[14]

A surface conclusion would assume the organizations cited are simply failing to adequately mobilize their people to deliver results. But, be very careful with that assumption. A litany of reasons may explain poor execution, but most likely, all can be traced back to the decisions and choices made during strategy design.

As I work with executive teams leading organizations of all sizes, I have a front-row seat to the frustrations, obstacles and traps executives and leaders face when it comes to getting strategy right.

Whether you're the owner of a small family manufacturing business, the CEO of a multi-billion-dollar global conglomerate, or the team leader of the five-person department that makes the home office hum, you need to ask yourself the **bolded** questions in the following sections. These questions are crafted to help you identify and address the sources of weak strategy execution plaguing your business.

I've divided the questions into two key categories: "people" and "process." As you read this section, recall the business formula that, if addressed, has the power to transform your organization:

Same People + Same Process = Same Results.

People

Let's start with *people*. When it comes to the "People" side of the equation above, the objective is to evaluate and realign your overall approach to support your strategy. Changing your approach to the people in your organization does not necessarily mean you need to "clean house" or replace current talent abruptly. What it does mean is that you must deliberately prepare and position your people to execute the strategy.

Under the "people" umbrella, there are three major areas that need alignment to strategy:

- Overall organizational structure (how you organize your people to execute the strategy)
- Overall talent makeup and cultural fit
- Overall leadership development

The following questions will help you self-assess the "People" side of the equation to achieve this calibration.

Do we possess a high-performance team?

As we've explored previously, your organization's ability to deliver beautiful, results-generating strategy is hugely dependent on leadership's commitment to designing, building and growing high-performance teams. And before organizations can build effective teams, they must first build *individuals*.

> *Before organizations can build effective teams, they must first build individuals.*

However, it's far too easy for leaders to be lulled into organizational silos, waiting too long to make necessary people changes, and missing opportunities to build a true team instead of just "filling positions." Every leader has become stuck in these ruts at some point in his or her career.

When was the last time you conducted a complete talent review of your entire team or organization? As your business has grown in its life cycle, have you evaluated whether or not you have the right talent and skill in critical roles?

You should also consider the values, mindset and attitudinal disposition of the people holding key roles. Do their hearts, minds and ambitions align with your vision for the organization?

Who is accountable for growth?

Business leaders need to find a way to keep growth at the forefront of the organization and ultimately, from slipping into the shadows of the day-to-day priorities. The current approach to strategy typically tasks functional leaders with figuring out where and how the organization will grow. While this has served well in the past, the fast moving external environment, coupled with unstable economic conditions and rapid entrepreneurial disruption, demands a new approach.

> *Lack of growth in our personal lives ultimately impedes professional growth.*

Organizations need to establish single accountability for driving a cohesive approach to strategy and growing the business unencumbered by political lines, territories or self-promotion. For a few ideas on how to do this in your organization, go back and read "The Secret Growth Strategy of the Ant Colony" in chapter 2.

Is personal growth on our radar?

Realizing that lack of growth in our personal lives ultimately impedes professional growth, and then doing something about it, could be the trigger point for leaders to start building the kind of cultures that perform consistently. Starting now, why not assume that *everyone* is accountable for owning personal growth? The research in this area is compelling and worth your time no matter what size organization you lead.

Does our organizational structure match our strategy and goals?

Many organizations insist on developing a strategy that works for their organization, instead of building an organization that works for their strategy. Do you see the big difference?

When football season is in gear, news headlines from across the NFL highlight the hiring of new coaches who bring new systems and new strategies to

> *Many organizations insist on developing a strategy that works for their organization, instead of building an organization that works for their strategy.*

their respective teams. These new strategies often require management to acquire new talent, possessing unique abilities and skills in specific positions, in order to be successful. To think the coaches would be able to execute a *new* system with the exact *same* talent and skill at every position is insanity.

Are you bold enough to make the changes needed to deliver the strategy? In order to release the organization's full potential as you pursue the new strategy, change is required. Organizations struggling with dismal strategy execution statistics are simply not making the tough staffing decisions required for success.

So, is the way you organize your employees working against, rather than in sync with, your growth goals? Ask yourself the following questions:

- Does our organizational structure add unnecessary friction or barriers to our people, preventing them from executing effectively?
- Is our structure (how we organize our employees) trapping or bottlenecking our capacity to achieve more?
- Does our talent investment align with or impede our strategic ambitions?
- Is the strategic and tactical know-how of our business "hidden" within the minds of a select few team members? Or do we have a plan to make that knowledge more transparent and communicate it to new or existing talent?
- Are we developing talent and systems in such a way where we don't need to rely too heavily on one or even a few individuals to drive our business?

Are our leaders creating more leaders?

Do we have a shortage of leadership? Are our current leaders encouraged to develop new leaders? Are they held accountable to do so?

Perhaps the widest capability gap that exists in any organization today is talent. And, unfortunately, in most organizations, the inability to identify and develop future leadership is pervasive. The "graying of corporate America" (which comprises the 40 percent of top leadership nearing retirement) will lead to numerous vacant seats on the organizational chart. Have you thought about who will fill those seats?

The leadership shortage conundrum runs much deeper than the annual "high-performer/high-potential" meeting you held a few years ago. It's a mindset that becomes part of your organization's DNA, and you need to hire accordingly. In other words, you should hire into your organization only proven leaders who have demonstrated the ability to develop, mentor, and grow others.

When it comes to executing strategy, this principle of 'growing leaders who grow other leaders' is the principle that receives the most talk, but the least action. Organizations that consistently perform at high levels inherently believe, with every fiber of their being, that the role of a leader is to create more leaders.

Are we inspiring our leaders, team members, and employees?

In my role as "Dad," I often get to witness coaching and leadership development at its finest—on the ball field or the basketball court. Recently, my son's coach highlighted a "best play" from our Saturday baseball game. The highlight was featured in the league's weekly newsletter:

A hard-hitting ball was sent to Landon Garretson on second base. He scooped up the ball as the first base runner sped toward him. Landon spun for the tag. He and the base runner collided in a tangle of arms, legs, and feet, falling to the ground. As the dust settled and the mess of arms and legs was unraveled, Landon Garretson was on his belly, in the dirt, empty glove to the left, still clutching the ball in his right hand ... and smiling! Amazingly, Landon was able to hold on to the baseball! The effort to achieve the second base out was remarkable. Kudos to Landon for his determination and relentless grip. In this play (collision!), Landon Garretson demonstrated a great example of courage and perseverance.

As Landon's dad, you can imagine how proud I was to see him not only experience this small success, but also be recognized for it.

> **People must grow before businesses grow.**

As I shared the league's write-up with Landon, I watched his originally lukewarm energy for the game transform into *red-hot drive*. His confidence level and his desire to get out and play soared as a result of the feedback.

Later that evening over dinner, we lifted our glasses of Crystal Light Green Tea to offer "cheers" for Landon on his accomplishment. "Cheers" is often how we recognize, celebrate, and encourage each other at home.

What about you? How do you set people on fire?

One of the truths of great organizations is that people must grow before businesses grow, and people are the heartbeat of your culture. Ongoing encouragement must be at the core of your organization's entire people-development effort.

> **Simply put, encouragement is the mechanism that shifts your culture into drive.**

Your culture is more than just the special difference you bring to the world; it also happens to be how you will execute your growth strategy. Simply put, encouragement is the mechanism that shifts your culture into drive.

People must grow before businesses grow.

When you recognize or encourage team members for specific accomplishments, it serves as confirmation that they *can*. I refer to this as "opening their can." Out of the can comes confidence. Confidence leads to a burning desire to go higher and further. It's a chain reaction.

Actually, there is one more link in that chain…

Something remarkable happens when you set someone on fire. It spreads. Landon's little brother, Lex, can't wait to get a baseball glove in his hands.

For more on how leaders can inspire and motivate their teams, be sure to read chapter 4.

Process

The second piece of our business formula addressing weak strategy execution focuses on *process*.

> **Same People + Same Process = Same Results.**

What exactly is process? *Dictionary.com* defines 'process' as "a systematic series of actions directed to some end."[15] The people in your organization must support your strategic goals through specific behaviors and activities, which constitute the "Process" part of the equation. How you identify, activate, and measure those activities is critically important to overall strategy execution, as you need to be continuously sharpening and/or modifying activities until they drive the results you desire.

Under the "Process" umbrella, there are three major dimensions you must align to strategy. Again, our objective is to calibrate these dimensions in alignment with where you want to *go*, as opposed to where you *are*:

- Specific activities and behaviors
- System for measuring, coaching, developing, and rewarding
- Operational rhythm or flow of business

The following questions will help you assess your business's processes as you address underperformance:

Do we have a strategy or a strategic plan?

Leaders that fall into this particular trap are guilty of running the engines and propellers before they've decided where to sail the ship. Putting the tactical in front of the strategy can lead to disaster. The ship ends up lost at sea and full of frustrated sailors.

> *Your strategy should define a strong value proposition for your target market. Your strategic plan should tell you the specific, tactical action steps and plans you will deploy to bring your strategy to life.*

Your strategy should define a strong value proposition for your target market, the distinctive capabilities you will activate to win in that market, and a picture of how you need to organize your business to make it happen.

Your strategic plan is, essentially, an instruction manual detailing the organization's overall strategy. Essentially, it should tell you the specific, tactical action steps and plans you will deploy to bring your strategy to life. It turns the strategy into specific actions.

Have you defined the precise activities (as well as the behaviors that support those activities) required to meet certain objectives as detailed in the strategic plan?

Have we connected our people and organization with our activities and processes in clear and logical ways?

Take a close, hard look at the intersection of people and process in the context of your strategic plan. Have you communicated clearly how the activities and behaviors, defined in your strategic plan, will allow you to accomplish your strategic objectives? Do your team members know which activities and behaviors they are accountable for—and perhaps more importantly, why?

Furthermore, how do your professional development systems line up? Does your performance management process align coaching, training and development to the right behaviors and activities?

Do we have ways of systematically evaluating, improving and reinforcing the results of our strategic plan?

Do you have a system in place to measure the effectiveness of the activities needed to deliver your strategy?

Do you have a system in place to review, calibrate, and refine activities regularly and deliver the right results?

Are you rewarding and offering incentives for the activities and behaviors that will drive your desired results?

Have we made new discoveries?

New discoveries often spur the need for new strategy. Every great strategy, business, or billion-dollar start-up success is traced back to a big learning or unearthing of opportunity. Whether it is a new product, service, technology, or experience, someone spent untold hours slaving over the target market to understand consumer needs and unexpressed wants.

If on-going learning and discovery is not part of the way you operate your business, it needs to be—or you run a big risk in being "out-discovered" by your competition. With the data-capturing capability available through real-time feedback platforms, organize your business to become intelligent. For more on how discovery drives the right strategy choice, review "Choosing the Right Growth Strategy for Your Business" in chapter 2.

> *If on-going learning and discovery is not part of the way you operate your business, it needs to be.*

And remember, big discovery fuels strategy.

What capability will we add or leverage?

They key word here is 'capability.' As I work with organizations, time and time again, I see scenarios in which leadership has identified opportunity to win shares in existing and new markets, but failed to complete (or even begin) the necessary research to understand the capabilities needed to win. Whether it's leveraging an existing core capability or building a new one, business leaders need to spend more time on this topic as it relates to strategy. Tactical efforts are falling short—and failing altogether—as companies try to expand their products and services only to discover they don't have the fire-power to get the job done.

Where will we place our bets?

Leaders are spreading resources too thinly across their portfolio of products or services instead of prioritizing and placing bets on a few products and services, allowing them to go "big and deep." Ultimately, spreading your organizational resources too thinly leads to a vicious cycle of believing lots of *little* initiatives will grow your entire portfolio. They won't. As you continue to chase so many "little" initiatives, you fall further behind the curve of your core businesses, which represent the largest percentage of your profit.

Are we simultaneously running *and* building?

Does running your business get in the way of building your business? Within your strategy process, you and your executive team must have open discussions regarding the best methods to run your business *and* build at the same time. Every company should be chasing a market *and* creating a new market simultaneously—in fact, it's the only way to ensure sustainable growth. Becoming an organization that can create, incubate and

> *Does running your business get in the way of building your business?*

build new ventures is not easy, but it is required to ensure organizational longevity.

I challenge you to review the information we've just covered. How many of the questions—both "people" and "process"—can you answer with an affirmative? In which areas do you have concerns? Did any of the questions jump off the page as topics or issues that have been on your radar and need addressing sooner rather than later?

> *Every company should be <u>chasing</u> a market and <u>creating</u> a new market simultaneously.*

As you calibrate your strategy, both your people *and* your processes must be considered. Strong strategy execution requires *both* and is at the heart of achieving record-breaking results. Failure to align these vital components undoubtedly results in individual and organizational underperformance.

As a leader, it's ultimately up to you and your executive team to uncover change opportunities that will lead to better execution—and that's exactly what it takes to remove '*same*' from the equation.

How to Know When You Have Strategy and Culture in Sync

So, we've assessed the people comprising your organization and the processes by which results are achieved. Now we must address the overall organizational culture of your business. But, which comes first? The strategy or the culture? When your organization was initially formed, did the strategy drive the culture? Or did the culture ultimately drive the strategic plans and direction of your company? And, which is more important? Your strategy or your culture? Finally, what or who has influenced your answers to these questions?

Starting today, I encourage you to think of strategy and culture as a *fusion, rather than two separate, mutually exclusive concepts.* A great visual is the canoe. If you've ever navigated a canoe down a winding, obstacle-heavy river, you know how important it is that the bow and the stern are synchronized.

Stay with me as we unpack this picture: Imagine the canoe as your organization and the river as the specific niche or industry in which you operate. Think of the paddler in the canoe's bow as your culture, providing power to your business. The canoe's stern is your strategy—requiring a steady guide to help navigate the vessel.

> *While culture defines how your organization will act, strategy tells you where you will end up if you collectively act "that way."*

When the bow and the stern (culture and strategy) are working together, the canoe is very effective in creating forward movement. Thus, while culture defines *how* your organization will act, strategy tells you *where you will end* up if you collectively act "that way."

Conversely, if you decide to put more weight in one end of the boat or the other, you're forced to rely on the river current, brute force and heroic acts to navigate the vessel. In an external environment littered with obstacles and unpredictability (like a river), you're likely to end up adrift or stuck. Trying to choose one without also focusing on the other is equally frustrating—in other words, if you don't have power, you're motionless, and if you are without steering, you are directionless.

Organizations that choose to address their organizational strategy and their internal business culture as two independent, mutually exclusive systems, usually experience disastrous results. Essentially, these organizations have chosen to put all of their organizational "weight" in one end of the boat or the other. This results in high turnover, leadership indecisiveness, customer churn, fear of the unknowns in the external environment, lack of execution, and—perhaps most importantly—stagnant revenue or profit growth (also known as "the plateau").

So, maybe it's time to grab the paddles. When there is is fusion between your organization's strategy and your internal culture, amazing things are bound to happen.

WORKBOOK

___

Chapter 3 Questions

Question: On a scale of 1 to 10 (10 being 'flawless'), how effective is your organization in executing your business strategy? List five reasons your strategy execution may be falling short.

_____

_____

_____

_____

_____

_____

_____

_____

_____

_____

_____

Question: Remember our important equation:

Same **People** + *Same* **Process** = *Same* **Results.**

Where side of the equation needs focus and prioritization in your business—people or process? Why?

_____

_____

_____

_____

_____

_____

_____

_____

_____

_____

_____

_____

_____

_____

_____

_____

_____

_____

_____

Question: Assess yourself and your executive team in terms of goal clarity, responsibility, accountability, and vulnerability. Which areas need the most improvement? How will you hold yourself and others accountable for improving in these areas?

_____

_____

_____

_____

_____

_____

_____

_____

_____

_____

_____

_____

_____

_____

_____

_____

_____

_____

_____

_____

Question: On a scale of 1 to 10 (10 being flawless), how effective is your leadership in creating more leaders? Is there a concrete plan in place to grow more leaders? Are leaders accountable (and rewarded) for growing more leaders? If not, why not?

_____
_____
_____
_____
_____
_____
_____
_____
_____
_____
_____
_____
_____
_____
_____
_____
_____
_____
_____
_____

Question: Is your business strategy in sync with your organization's culture? Do you treat strategy and culture as mutually exclusive? In your organizational canoe, where do you place more "weight"—on your strategy or on your culture?

_____

_____

_____

_____

_____

_____

_____

_____

_____

_____

Circle Back: It all comes down to execution! Review the questions in "Why Your Strategy Isn't Working" to identify and address weaknesses in strategy execution. Are you using the _same people_ and the _same process_ but expecting _different_ results? In particular, focus on growing more leaders who can help execute strategy effectively—leaders with goal clarity, leaders willing to take responsibility and accountability, and leaders who show vulnerability. Together with your leadership team, get your strategy and culture in sync so they complement each other for maximum effectiveness and growth.

CHAPTER FOUR

Growing Above and Beyond:
Foundations of Growth-Driven Leadership

Most of us spend the bulk of our days being inundated with information—from our colleagues, friends, and family, but most of all from our smartphones, computers, and televisions. The flood of information can be near-overwhelming at times.

But sometimes one clear voice rises above the clamor—and when that happens, it can be a game-changer.

The One Leadership Book Everyone Should Read

If you've read a few shelves worth of leadership books throughout you career (as I have!) it's quite possible you've been exposed to hundreds of different theories, meanings, and opinions on the broad topic of leadership. Thousands of leadership titles in airport bookstores, Barnes and Noble, and Amazon.com's endless virtual "bookshelves" have, ironically, left many people more confused and conflicted about what leadership really is, what it looks like, and more importantly, how to put it in action in our lives and careers.

Through of all my years as a student, coach, teacher, and practitioner of leadership, however, never have I come across a book as compelling as Perry Noble's *The Most Excellent Way to Lead.*[16]

Perry Noble is the founding pastor of NewSpring Church, based in South Carolina, one of the fastest growing churches in the United States. Over the last decade, NewSpring Church has expanded in several locations across the state. Noble is not only a gifted

> *Boastful people are bitter people. Humble people, however, are hungry people.*

writer, but also one of the most compelling communicators I've heard.

In my opinion, no other book or resource sets the topic of leadership straight more than Perry Noble's book. Perry's words captured both my heart and my head. I only wish the book had been available when I started my career. When it comes to leadership, this will be the first book—and perhaps the only book—I will have my four children read.

Noble's case for the most excellent way to lead is rooted in the Bible. In 1 Corinthians 12:31, Paul writes, "I will show

> *Our goal isn't to make much of ourselves; instead we're to make much of the people we're leading.*

you a still more excellent way" (ESV). Noble states, "If we practice leadership (regardless of who, what or where we lead) in the way that Jesus did, we will become leaders other people want to follow."

Not only does Noble's book illuminate the foundational truth behind leadership, but it also provides a clear roadmap and reference for the reader as he or she puts the principles into action.

> *I believe God always wants more for us than we want for ourselves.*

While I won't spoil the book for you, I do want to share these six quick leadership "nuggets" from *The Most Excellent Way to Lead:*

Boastful people are bitter people. Humble people, however, are hungry people. They know there's more to be done. They don't mind washing feet and they don't have to be the center of attention.

A call to lead is a call to serve and sacrifice. Our goal isn't to make much of ourselves; instead we're to make much of the people we're leading. Only then will we become leaders worth following.

One of the worst things we can do as leaders is subject the people for whom we're responsible to small, safe ideas. I believe God always wants more for us than we want for ourselves. I believe one of the best questions a leader in any field can ask God when they experience success is, "What now, Lord?"

> *When we allow the voices of those who know us the least to shape us the most, we are in serious trouble.*

Critics want to make a point while coaches want to make a difference. When we allow the voices of those who know us the least to shape us the most, we are in serious trouble.

Sometimes you need opportunities more than resources. When it comes to solving problems, Perry Noble conditions his team to "not immediately think that more resources are needed, but rather that they've been given more opportunities to be creative and to be great stewards of all that's been placed in our hands."

If you spend all your effort trying to make sure everything is completely fair (whether as a leader or follower), you are setting yourself up for disappointment. Noble goes on to say, "Fair is a place where you ride rides." How perfect! (And, for the record, this is one statement my wife and I repeat to our children ad-nauseam).

> *The most excellent way to lead is also the most difficult.*

Most of all, I appreciate the way Perry Noble chose to conclude his book: "Instead of approaching leadership the way the world does, with a hunger for power and self-advancement and competition, may you see that the best style of leadership is *love*."

Here's the big challenge: the most excellent way to lead is also the most difficult.

Are you up to it?

Which Kind of Leadership Describes You?

As Noble's book suggests, to reach your full potential as a leader, you must give some serious thought to the *outcome* of leadership.

If you've never pondered this, then pause here and give it 30 seconds of thought. When you think about the 'outcome of leadership,' what words, thoughts, and images immediately come to mind?

> *The outcome of leadership is <u>growth</u>. Period.*

This very question has caused my mind to do some serious somersaults recently, and I've come to this realization: the outcome of leadership is *growth*. Period.

And *growth* happens to be at the heart of the "forward movement" we seek to build in organizations, teams, and individuals everywhere.

While the outcome of leadership should always be growth, there are typically two kinds of leaders that emerge in most organizations. Your organization needs both kinds of leaders—and lots of them!

The "Spark"

The first kind of leader is wild and crazy about starting something new. From building businesses to building roads, this leader is typically blazing the trail in front of the rest of the team. 'Spark' describes a leader who lights the inspiration for a new product, a change in attitude, an idea, or a business. This leader embraces the vision and runs with it, enlisting and influencing others to action.

Consider Steve Jobs of Apple, with the iPod followed by the iPhone—the spark is lit and before you know it, mini-fires are burning all over the organization quickly spreading into a full-fledged blaze.

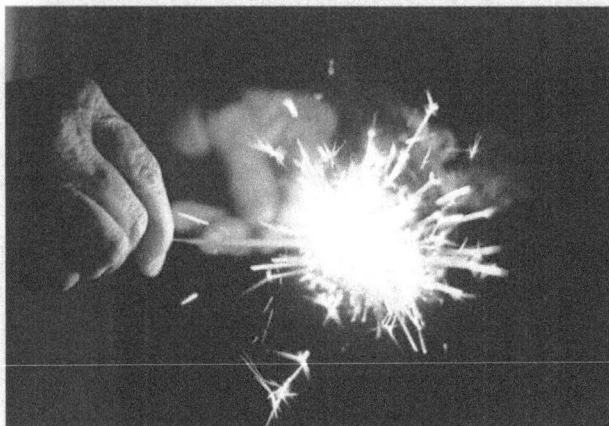

What's the spark famous for?

That's what the spark is famous for. This kind of leader ignites and fuels a new direction or vision. The spark remains fired up and burning bright, moving on only to light the spark again. Here's the good news: everyone can be a spark for something!

The "Fire-Builder"

The second kind of leader is the leader who can fan the spark into a flame and eventually build it into a blaze of beauty. The fire-builder is extremely skilled at knowing what kind of logs the fire needs, how many, when to throw them on the blaze and how to keep the fire from burning out of control. Anybody can be a fire-builder—it's up to you to step forward and be intentional about bringing your leadership to whatever needs building. The beauty in both types of leaders is that they depend on (and need!) each other: fire-builders need a spark—just as the spark needs a fire-builder.

> *Everyone wants a meaningful quest. And, to know exactly the special contribution they make to a special group of people seeking to make a special difference.*

So, let me ask you: Does the visual imagery of the "spark" or "fire" change how you view leadership? And, perhaps most important, what kind of leader do you aspire to be? One thing is for certain: both kinds of leaders possess a deep-burning passion for growth.

Don't wait for the position, the title, or the phone call. Go start a fire. Go build a fire. Now.

The Gift Everyone Wants

In December 2015, Delta Airlines announced they were banning *it* from their flights.[17] News stations across the US reported battery issues and the propensity for *it* to catch fire. And, Amazon began urging customers to dispose of *it* due to safety concerns.

So, what exactly was *it*?

Apparently, *it* was the hottest and hardest-to-find gift of the 2015 holiday season: the hover board. While young (and some older) folks across America glided—often dangerously—along neighborhood streets, manufacturers moved on, quickly pursuing the next big "it" gift. They replaced *it* with even newer fads and hot-ticket items, leaving the board to collect dust in garages across America.

Any idea what is even more wished-for than the trendiest holiday gifts? Three little words: *a compelling vision*. Yes, the most requested wish at the top of everyone's list is *a vision*. And as a leader, it's your responsibility to help supply that vision for your organization.

> *We are all born with a deeply wired DNA to create value for others.*

What people really want is something to chase. An aim. Something to be. A purpose and a "why." A meaningful quest. And to know exactly the special contribution they make to a special group of people seeking to make a special difference.

It's that simple. And it costs nothing.

We are all born with a deeply wired DNA to create value for others, whether it be for family, friends, coworkers or customers. What this means is that we each know precisely the special gifts and strengths that are God-given and how they add value to a bigger purpose in our lives.

In a list of habits that drive happiness, expert neuroscientist Alex Korb says that "thinking about long-term goals can release dopamine, the neurotransmitter that makes us feel better and more motivated about what we want to achieve."[18]

A compelling vision answers our calling to become something *more*. Vision is the state of *becoming*. The reason we use the word 'becoming' is that a vision does not exist unless it's committed-to or acted-on in some fashion. 'Becoming' transforms vision from a mere statement to a verb—an *action*.

How About "What If?"

But where does this path of action—the vision—begin?

What if you pulled your team together in a quiet coffee shop, taking deliberate time creating (or re-crafting) your vision and reminding them why they exist? What if you asked them what they are becoming or are seeking to become? Without a vision, they may have difficulty answering these questions.

What if the next time you spend one-on-one time with your team members, you help them craft a vision for their lives? What if it were as simple as helping them see a future picture of *what* or *who* they might become. What if you helped them see more clearly the special talents they possess and how they contribute to the big picture? Ask them if they'll answer the call.

Leaders, there's no better way to spend your time. As a leader, you're blessed with the gift of vision. Isn't now the perfect time to give it away?

And the underpinnings behind all compelling visions is the question of "why." With this in mind, let's explore the importance of the story behind your vision.

So ... What's Your Story?

A few summers ago, while visiting the Jersey Shore, my wife and my oldest daughter spotted an interesting stone that had washed up along the shoreline. They used the sharp edge of the stone to carve the letters of our last name in the sand. Garretson. They took a picture of their handiwork, and we filed it away with all of the other family vacation mementos. As I flipped through the beach pictures recently, this image of our last name carved in sand stopped me dead in my tracks.

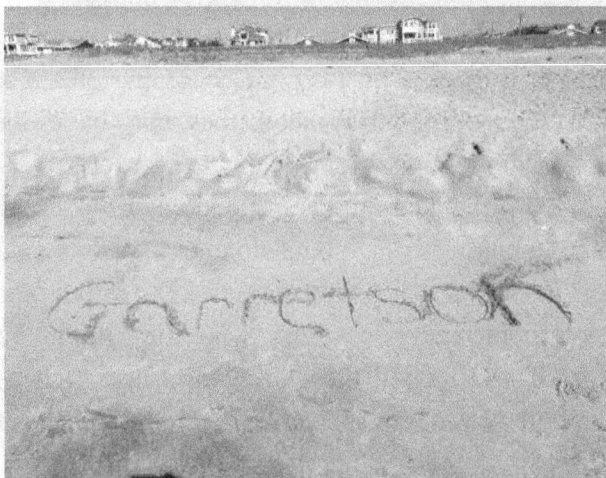

What's the story behind the name?

And it should. There is a story behind that name. It communicates my values and beliefs, as well as the kind of leadership I bring to initiatives, teams and organizations. It's who I am. As we learn more about who our leaders are, we not only build a stronger personal connection to them, but we glean specific insight as to the "why" behind their leadership.

Not until you learn that Michael Jordan was cut from his freshman high school basketball team do you begin to understand what fuels the intense competitiveness and desire to win that propelled him to the pinnacle of the sport. Jordan's under-privileged upbringing—the backyard hoop-in-the-dirt where he shot baskets for hours—tells even more about the kind of work ethic he possesses. Only when we understand Jordan's upbringing and his fierce work ethic can we appreciate how much he expected of his teammates and the competitiveness he brought to every practice and every game.

> *Here's the problem: most leaders attempt to communicate a vision while failing to communicate their leadership story.*

Here's the problem: most leaders attempt to communicate a vision while failing to communicate their leadership *story*. Therefore, the people they lead never really know who their leaders *are* at the very core. Until a leader communicates his or her leadership story, employees only know the name on the email in their inbox, the placard on the wall outside the office, or the list of priorities rattled off in morning meetings.

My Leadership Story

From a very young age, I remember my mom and dad dragging my little brother and me to our family manufacturing business on Saturdays while they both tended to business that needed handling. My brother and I learned the family business from the ground up. From the time I could walk, I remember helping my mom and dad sweep floors, stock shelves, and pack and ship products to customers. I (not so fondly) remember packing boxes in the factory during the hot Pennsylvania summers with no air conditioning. I was raised to value commitment, hard work and honesty.

Many hot summers, diplomas, and degrees later, my brother and I finally (somehow) graduated out of the factory and into the air-conditioned office area, where we were awarded desks in a cubicle and were tasked to sift through miles of "green bar" sales reports while we pounded out data, charts, and graphs. This was *way* before

> *After marrying my wife and eventually becoming "Dad" to four children, I became focused on chasing another kind of potential: my children's.*

salesforce.com, fancy MacBooks, and even smartphones. Officially joining my father's family business full-time, I completely entrenched myself in what became a 24-hour-a-day, 365-day-a-year "mission to the top."

With an intense desire to be productive and make an impact, I laddered through a number of sales and marketing leadership roles within the family business, and later climbed many rungs on the Fortune 500 ladder.

In my climb to the top, I finally found the rung on the ladder that fit. I discovered that my true passion—and where I excelled most—was in the one-on-one time I spent with employees and customers educating, coaching, consulting and advising them on strategies to improve and grow. Those kinds of interactions just seemed to work—and produced results. On that rung of the ladder, I could immediately see the wider circle of potential around customers' businesses and relished crafting the plan to help them realize their potential.

My wife and our four children.

After marrying my wife and eventually becoming "Dad" to four children, I became focused on chasing another kind of potential: *my children's*. Rooting my family in a strong faith and instilling that faith as a priority over their lives completes the tightly woven fabric of strong values that characterizes *my* leadership.

That's the story behind the name *Garretson*.

Now, I must work every day to instill those values in those I lead, whether through client engagements, consulting, advising, writing, or speaking—or most importantly, with my kids.

The Challenge

How will you use *your* story to impact the people in your circle?

I know you have the aspiration to grow or you wouldn't be reading this book. The single most important thing you can do right now is to share your leadership story so others will know who you are.

> *The single most important thing you can do right now is to share your leadership story so others will know who you are.*

So, what's the story behind who you are as a person and a leader?

Whatever you do, don't forget to share that story with those closest to you.

The Vulnerability of the Valleys

As you think about your story, take care to also remember—and share—the valleys.

Regardless of industry or organizational size, business owners and executives across the globe tell me they lack the right talent at the right time, their strategy and structure are misaligned, and they are unable to deliver meaningful innovation to the marketplace. Additionally, executive management is frustrated by their organizations' failure to drive the personal and professional growth of their employees adequately.

But there is an even bigger, less-mentioned (and often ignored) challenge that has a strangling grip on the necks of our teams, organizations and families, silently and slowly suffocating growth potential. That strangling grip is a pervasive *lack of trust*.

> *From building families to building businesses, trust is a foundational pillar that must be rock-solid.*

From building families to building businesses, trust is a foundational pillar that must be rock-solid. Before you can put more floors on the building, you need a foundation that can handle the pressure. Thus, lack of trust is a huge barrier to growth.

> *Lack of trust is a huge barrier to growth.*

The problem is that most leaders will not accept or admit there is a lack of trust within their businesses or between customers or team members.

So, what can be done to ensure this pillar does not crumble under the pressure of growth?

There is a great deal that can be done to build trust, from off-site team building workshops to tactical strategies including better communication and consistency in policy and procedures. And while these are all important and impactful, there is one rare characteristic that leads to deep, foundation-building, virtually unshakeable trust—and that characteristic is found in the valleys.

The Valleys of Life

As I've said before, growth never happens on the top of the mountain. It happens in the valleys. This is not only true of nature, but also true of people, teams, organizations, and even, families. It's the valleys of life where transformation happens. In the valleys is where the growth stories emerge—which is why you can't leave out the valleys when you tell your story.

> *Growth never happens on the top of the mountain. It happens in the valleys.*

Everyone has experienced valleys in their lifetime—both personal and professional hardships that led to new direction and unexpected growth. Leaders need to better leverage the valleys they've experienced to inspire and encourage the people they lead. My personal experience is that most people find the valleys of life to be shameful, making every effort to hide them while enduring the journey, and forever banishing each valley from their memory once the trial is finally over.

However, what we don't realize is that we are surrounded by people who are currently in a valley right now—struggling with some aspect of their life that is impeding their potential.

Your story of surviving the valley can serve as a climbing rope to help others out of their own valleys. When you share your story, you create a safe place for others to open up about their own dark places. Your story, like a rope of rescue, can reach them in their valleys and provide all the hope they need. Watch

> *Most people find the valleys of life to be shameful, making every effort to hide them.*

them grab the rope; watch them begin to grow anew. Not only could you release someone from their valley, but the transformation and growth that result could also impact others in a chain reaction.

Five Steps to Foster Healthy Vulnerability

The act of sharing life in the valley is also known as vulnerability. And ultimately, this kind of vulnerability leads to a deeper connection with each other and results in a cement-like trust within your inner circles.

Incredible power is harnessed when we demonstrate vulnerability. In a compelling TED Talk from Brené

> *The act of sharing life in the valley is also known as vulnerability.*

Brown, she defines 'vulnerability' as allowing ourselves to be seen, possessing uncommon courage to be imperfect, and a willingness to let go of who we think we should be in order to be

who we are.[19]

So, how exactly, do we forge this kind of vulnerability? How do we, as leaders, bring it to life in our organizations and teams—and maybe more importantly, in our families?

There are five steps needed to leverage your valleys for the benefit of other people in your life:

1. Open up. While not an easy chore by any stretch of the imagination, the first step in building vulnerability is opening up. You and I need to be transparent and honest about where, how and why we have failed or how we have been dealt a difficult hand. It could be in the form of job loss, addiction, medical or health challenges, financial hardships, fractured relationships—the list goes on. Whatever it is, make sure to detail the hardship, pain and hopelessness that you felt on the journey.

> *Vulnerability is a willingness to let go of who we think we should be in order to be who we are.*

Personally, showing vulnerability has been a challenge for me. I've had to work hard at sharing my valleys, and it has taken a great deal of courage and confidence to open up. In particular, a corporate restructuring many years ago led to a job loss at the same time we were adopting a baby girl. It was one of the deepest and widest valleys for both me and my family. Little did we know, God was getting ready to work in our life as He never had before. (More on that later in the book.)

There is an even bigger opportunity to share our mistakes and valley experiences with our children. When we do, we teach them not only how to respond to life's disappointments, but also that God made us all imperfect so that He could send us a Savior. After all, our kids know better than anyone else that Mommy and Daddy make mistakes, too!

2. Share the transformation. Sharing how you were able to pick yourself up when you were lying flat on your back, get back on the path, and climb out of the valley is the inspiration others need for hope. Everyone has a story of transformation, and many people experience it in the darkest of times. Specifically, share how you climbed out of the valley, and how it changed you.

3. Challenge. If you've told your story well, then others will feel safe and comfortable sharing their personal stories in turn. And when they do, and you have listened intently, you—as a leader—are in a position to challenge them. Encourage them to grow while also helping them see the value of their time spent in the valley.

During my valley experience, the time I spent reflecting and praying was absolutely critical to my own journey—and to eventually climbing out of the abyss. Focusing my prayers on my family, and on the ways God wanted to use me, opened doors and provided clarity in ways I never thought possible.

4. Encourage. While sharing your valley story could be the spark others need, please make no mistake: it will be your *ongoing encouragement* that will ultimately fuel their growth, propelling them to keep going.

Replace 'Executive' in Chief Executive Officer with 'Encouragement' and you become the Chief Encouragement Officer. And everyone needs one of those.

5. Unlock potential in others. If transformation and growth happen in the darkest valleys of life, it sort of makes a trip to the valley worth it, doesn't it? Think of vulnerability as a key to unlock potential in others. Your story is the key. Don't be afraid to tell it!

The Power of Vulnerability

As an executive coach, I've come to view vulnerability as the ultimate level high-performing teams and families must strive to achieve. Rarely, however, do I see organizations or leadership who've mastered the concept. Brené Brown, as referenced earlier, highlights the *power* of vulnerability. Brown defines 'vulnerability,' in part, as allowing oneself to be seen, and ultimately, this 'being seen' is what leads to connection with others. She reminds us how societal pressures have conditioned us to drive for an unattainable state of controlling, predicting, and perfecting.[20]

Brown speaks to an uncommon courage to be imperfect and a willingness to let go of who we think we *should b*e in order to be who we *really are*.

While Brown does not specifically tie vulnerability to trust in her presentation, I believe an unwillingness to show vulnerability is what keeps under-performing teams from ever achieving the kind of trust that high-performance teams possess.

Pridefully masking insecurities and imperfections often leads to gossip and politics within teams, not to mention a tendency to overcommit and exaggerate capabilities; this can lead to foundational cracks in trust.

However, being real about who we are, imperfections and all, will reveal where the gaps lie in our own lives and in our teams. We not only uncap the potential for new growth in our personal lives, but we also enlist the support of our inner circles to cheer us on.

I realize this all sounds a bit idealistic; indeed, vulnerability is one of the real "hard-to-do's" in life. But dream with me! Let's define how we could build more vulnerability in our lives. If nothing else, we can take small steps toward relenting in our pride and accepting our imperfection—and this can unleash new levels of

> *Virtually everything of real meaning or significance requires not only effort and commitment, but also an investment of time.*

joy, contentment, and growth in ourselves, our teams, and most importantly, our children.

Ask yourself the following questions, and take time to contemplate your answers:

- Have you ever been a member of a team (personal or organizational) that willingly displayed a meaningful level of vulnerability with each other or with customers?
- If so, what were some of the keys or strategies employed to build vulnerability?

- How about with your family? Have you been successful in fostering vulnerability with your family? How did you do it?

Three Areas Where Leaders Must Be Extra-Deliberate with Their Time

It's been said that nothing worthwhile is ever accomplished overnight. Virtually everything of real meaning or significance requires not only effort and commitment, but also an investment of time. In particular, it's really the small investments of time over a longer period of time that add up to something significant.

If those assumptions are true, in what areas of your life, personally, is it most difficult to make up for lost time? Where in your life is it almost impossible to put on a rally hat and expect a late, fourth-quarter comeback or a 48-hour marathon is possible?

This discussion was part of a personal growth series called "Ask It," written and delivered by Andy Stanley, pastor of NorthPoint Church in Alpharetta, Georgia. The series explores the idea that "small deposits of time, over time" impact our progress in areas of life that matter most such as our health and our relationships. And, where we fail to make those precious investments of time, it's not only next to impossible to "catch-up," but we also subject ourselves to less-than-desirable consequences.[21]

Over a long flight, not only did the topic weigh on my mind personally, but I also began to consider how this phenomenon plays out in organizations and with leaders. In what areas of organizational life is it most difficult to make up for lost time? Asked differently, what areas of the business need steady, incremental investments of time, over time, in order to make a positive difference?

> *The biggest investments you can make for your organization are the small increments of time, new experiences and opportunities you allocate for the next-level leaders.*

There are three areas in particular in which leaders must be deliberate in investing small amounts of time, over time, or they put their organization in a vulnerable and risky position.

1. Leadership Development

The mission of all great leadership is to create more leaders. Period. As a leader you are called to develop and grow people, at whatever cost—even if it's time. The biggest investments you can make for your organization are the small increments of time, new experiences and opportunities you allocate for the next level leaders. When it comes to developing next-level leaders, most organizations wait far too long, and they are inevitably caught scurrying to replace lost talent to avoid a drop in performance.

There are four keys to staying on track in regard to leadership development:

- A thorough knowledge of who the emerging or next-level leaders are across the organization through periodic talent reviews
- Each and every leader taking accountability to "own" the development plan for those next-level leader(s)
- Next-level leaders engaged in development activity and assignments on a weekly basis
- A "gaps" meeting to identify progress with leadership development activity

2. Team Building

Building a team is far from being the classic all-nighter project, right? Turning a 'department' into a 'team' will require a steady investment of time together—quite possibly months and years. This has become a much more difficult feat in today's mobile, virtually-connected world where individuals are spread throughout the globe. Building a great business team is so much more than getting the right talent in the right roles.

A solid team can hold each other accountable, be vulnerable with each other, function cohesively and collaboratively across functions, and exhibit a balanced make-up in style, approach and personality.

There are four keys to staying on track when it comes to team building:

- Top leaders must be tuned-in to team performance and engagement across the organization
- Each leader must be accountable for and "own" his or her team-development plan
- At least one team-development activity should occur weekly, with additional development activities and assignments occurring quarterly
- A "gaps" meeting should be held regularly to identify team-development progress

3. Coaching, Training, and Development

Coaching, training, and development is the third area where incremental, regular inputs of time truly matter. A 2014 *Forbes* article entitled, "Spending on Corporate Training Soars: Employee Capabilities Now a Priority" states that "more than 70% of organizations cite 'capability gaps' as one of their top five challenges, but many companies also tell us that it takes 3–5 years to take a seasoned professional and make them fully productive."[22] If you're not investing in repetitive training and development initiatives for your entire staff—top to bottom—you're putting your business in a vulnerable position.

There are four keys to staying on track when it comes to coaching, training, and development:

- Your organization should have a comprehensive coaching system in place. Individual coaching (linked to organizational strategic goals), should occur, in some form, on a *weekly* basis.

- The coaching system should identify capability and performance gaps and should address those gaps with training.
- Leadership should hold regular "gaps" meetings to assess organizational learning and development strategies.
- Training initiatives must be steady, consistent and regular, as opposed to one-time events.

Did you catch the emphasis on the word *weekly* above? Leadership, team, and individual development should be happening on a weekly basis.

I wouldn't be surprised if more than half of all organizations aren't lagging behind in at least one of these areas. In today's fast-paced marketplace, it's far too easy to let short-term pressures rule the day. Before you know it, you look up and wonder where the weeks and months have gone. Worse yet, one glance at your calendar can leave you shaking your head, wondering where you've spent your time.

So, I'm curious. What does all of this look like for you and your organization? Have I missed any areas that leaders should have on their watch-list when it comes to making sure they are making small investments of time, over time? Could you choose one area where you need to be more deliberate in investing small amounts of time, over time?

While it's always hard to find *more* time—especially when it comes to the seemingly unurgent matters of leadership development, team building, and coaching—be very careful, as these are the areas where the consequences of *not* spending incremental time not only cripple your organization, but also debilitate the very people who run your organization.

The Best Coaching Session You'll Ever Have

While we're on the topic of coaching, let's turn the tables a bit. I've found the best coaching sessions always teach me something new about myself—whether I like the lesson or not!

Have you ever experienced this kind of coaching session?

The awkwardness that accompanies these kinds of coaching conversations is enough to make leaders—regardless of job title or job level—shudder. Digging beneath the surface can be uncomfortable. But it's ex-

> *The seeds need the rain to sprout and build strong roots. Your people need coaching conversations to expand their abilities and deliver results.*

actly what's needed to trigger big growth events in you and in your people, and ultimately what drives forward movement in your organization.

So, why don't we have more conversations like these more often in organizations?

Perhaps what is needed is not another coaching session template, but instead a coaching *system* that truly integrates coaching into the culture and operating rhythm of the organization. Over time, the system should foster mini-conversations (as opposed to that one-time, dreadful event) that occur more often, in real-time, as the team is engaged in executing the growth strategy.

Spurring these conversations throughout the organization is akin to rainfall on new seed. The seeds need the rain to sprout and build strong roots. Your people need coaching conversations to expand their abilities and deliver results.

> *People growth drives organizational growth. If you have a desire to see your people grow, they need rainfall more than once or twice a year.*

I am not advising against formally planned coaching or review sessions in organizations. Regular performance reviews are absolutely necessary. I am not suggesting you micro-manage your staff. And I am not suggesting that a coaching system negates the need for "getting the right people in the right seats."

What I am suggesting is that people growth drives organizational growth. If you have a desire to see your people grow, they need rainfall more than once or twice a year.

If more than 70 percent of strategies fail due to poor execution, wouldn't it be worth having a coaching system that will drive better coaching sessions, and consequently, strengthen your execution?

Left untouched, bad habits only become worse. Consequently, we end up further from our vision, often facing new obstacles that require heroic efforts to recover.

Do you have an effective coaching system in your business? Is it integrated into your growth strategy? If you could re-design a better coaching system for your organization, what's one thing you would change?

Let me rephrase that last question: If you were a seed—getting ready to explode with growth—what would you crave?

The very best coaching sessions occur around and inside cultures that possess the right coaching systems. Coaching systems at strong organizations share the following three attributes:

- Coaching is linked inextricably to a growth strategy (this is rare).
- Leadership believes its purpose is to create more leaders (this is *very* rare).
- Coaching is a hardwired habit, as opposed to a dreaded chore (this is *extremely* rare).

Here's how these three attributes can make a difference:

Coaching—Inextricably Linked to a Growth Strategy

A growth strategy is the ultimate starting point for your organization and it must be visited over and over again. Think of your growth strategy as an outward-looking development plan for your organization where you're continually surfacing new opportunity to create value for markets and customers. Consequently, these value creation opportunities often require organizations to build new capabilities. New capabilities require new organizational structures, as well as developing and choosing people to activate the new strategy.

When an organization decides it's going to grow in new and different ways, it has an amazing ripple effect on how and when people need to be developed. Team members must be developed *before* the changes in order to support the new strategy. If you and I were going to add floors on top of an existing house, we would most likely be faced with critical adjustments to the foundation to support the taller house.

If done properly, a growth strategy will resolve this trap, once and for all.

Growth-centered organizations are constantly shaping and forming their businesses not only to position themselves as the best version, but they are also in a perpetual state of "becoming." Subsequently, the same is true of their leaders and teams.

In these kinds of organizations, leaders spend an inordinate amount of time reinforcing the unique talent, skills and gifts of individual performers, explaining why those performers have been chosen for a certain role, and expressing confidence in the abilities of those performers to drive the business forward. Leadership continually revisits revisit the "why" aspect of the teams' roles, tying their jobs back to broader growth strategy choices, including markets served, target customers, and the unique value they deliver.

Leadership Believes Its Purpose Is to Create More Leaders

Leaders in growth-centered organizations are focused on building more leaders. They believe their efforts to build people, customers and value directly effects growth in revenue and profit, not the reverse. This is easy to say but extremely difficult to act on— especially if you commonly find your organization in a series of reaction-oriented cycles involving mad-dashes to chase short-term numbers.

> *Leaders in growth-centered organizations are focused on building more leaders.*

When organizations are intentional about creating a culture that builds future leaders, awesome coaching experiences naturally follow.

Often, coaching conversations in growth-centered businesses uncover areas impeding performance or abilities to lead. Possible obstacles include blind-spot personality traits that hinder performance or leadership effectiveness; office-home life challenges; lack of opportunity or missed opportunities to collaborate horizontally or vertically; and countless others.

These are the kinds of conversations that trigger big growth events in your people, but they only happen on the watches of leaders who see their legacy in the people they leave behind.

Coaching Is a Hardwired Habit, Not a Dreaded Chore

When leaders create the right kinds of conversations with people in their organizations, they're building a *relationship* where a commitment to the follow-up process is taken seriously. Through real-time, mini-coaching sessions integrated into the operating rhythm of the business, leaders are consistently partnering with their people to drive organizational development forward— almost like a college basketball coach stepping a player aside to provide in-the-moment counsel after an emotional outburst that resulted in a technical foul.

Creating this kind of high-performing, people-centered organization is much easier than you think. And it all starts with the right growth strategy and leadership DNA at the top of the business. It will be in that kind of organization where you and those you are leading will experience the best coaching sessions of your life.

Four Salty Leadership Lessons from the Beach

Of course, learning doesn't occur only when you're at work. Even vacations can sometimes help you understand growth in ways that are relevant back in the workplace.

As I reflect on a recent family vacation—involving a week of 105-degree or hotter days with eleven family members (six under the age of ten) packed into one beach house, juggling different sleep schedules, nap times, food interests, and snack preferences—I smile (sort of) as I remember having to endure a spectrum of emotions, noise and chaos.

Interestingly and unexpectedly, however, there were four lessons that emerged beneath the chaos of that vacation—lessons not only valuable for "next time" but also, lessons that served fresh perspective on leadership in the workplace.

If you've ever had the great fortune of getting smacked in the face with an ocean wave, as my four children have experienced several times, then you have first-hand recollection of the rapid, burning rush that stretches down your throat as a giant gulp of seawater pours into your mouth. It's salty. And it burns.

I'm giving you fair warning: the four lessons below are "salty." They will burn inside. Maybe you will burn with regret as I did, agreeing that you've missed opportunities to lead.

1. The ovens need to cool down.

You've likely been there—multiple families in one house trying to organize meals, activities, and events for an entire week, with too many chefs in the kitchen pushing separate agendas and opinions, often leading to moments of contention, disagreement, and frustration.

Things can become heated emotionally and relationally very quickly. It's not uncommon—and not pleasant.

Think of times in the office or even at home when the pressure of a strained relationship, a decision, or a disagreement hijacks emotions. If you have your emotion-radar on, you can immediately sense a change in tone—in voice, body language or mood—that sends an internal notification that something is not right.

Regardless of fault, trying to repair a relational gap or reach a difficult decision can't be done in the heat of the moment. If you open the oven while it's still hot, you'll get burned every time. As leaders, walking away from a heated moment to "let the oven cool down" is the secret sauce to making sound decisions and effectively addressing relational barriers.

2. Connect with each one (not everyone).

This should be a new term in Webster's: 'each one.' Vacations are about connecting with *each one*, not *everyone*. Too often as leaders (both at home and in the office), we generalize our desire to connect with everyone. We bring teams together for lunch on Friday or big dinners on the last night of vacations with entire families.

While certainly difficult at times, what people (including children) need most from a leader is one-on-one time. A week spent vacationing with four children and your spouse will certainly keep you busy trying to carve out individual time with each family member, but it *is* worth it! What your family and team needs, first and foremost, is a leader who connects with *each* one—not everyone at once.

Skip the big dinners and build one-on-one time into your vacation or work calendar now. It's the kind of long-term investment that will pay big dividends years from now.

During that same extended family vacation in the crowded beach house, we celebrated our boys' summer birthdays. All four of the kids have become very skilled at strategically hovering during the present-opening ceremony to find the one gift that the birthday kid does not appear interested in—and then become quick to snatch it and run!

This year's "snatch and run" gift for my oldest daughter was the Connect Four game.

Connect Four teaches raw strategy. And it's easy—you can play it with your children. The game challenged my daughter to continually zoom in and zoom out. She needed to be able to move quickly from seeing the *whole* board to drilling down to her *next move*, and then calculating possible responses to certain moves I might make, and even looking two steps ahead.

We had an absolute blast playing that game together. Not only is it a great strategy-teaching game, but also an opportunity for me to spend one-on-one time with my children. And yes, I know, there is an app now for Connect Four. We are not interested. We choose to connect instead.

3. Communicate to terminate.

Our family vacation reminded me of the importance of communication. The most common and perhaps damaging mistake leaders make is failing to communicate. Often leaders make assumptions about how people (team members and customers alike) should think, feel, or behave and when they don't, leaders are often quick to grow frustrated and upset. Over time, if not proactive, a person's failure to meet the leader's assumptions about how he or she should act can begin to build up—kind of like termites eating away at the foundation of a house. Before long, the damage is irreparable.

Our vacation week was littered with little "termites" that could have been terminated with better communication, including what time we were leaving for the beach or which restaurant we would be dining at each night.

When you put the microscope on your individual and team relationships at home or at the office, are there termites present?

Communicate to terminate. People need clear, consistent, and constant communication to stay in lock step with each other, regardless of the leadership scenario. You need to be proactive and assertive with expectations of others in order to create the kind of growing relationships that are the mark of great organizations and teams.

4. Make memories.

Vacationing with the family is all about making memories, right? Whether beach ball-sized snow cones, trips to an out-of-state urgent care, or late-night bike rides, everybody leaves vacation week with a special memory—and, as you might expect, multiple electronic devices in "memory overload" with photos and videos from the week.

When we return from vacation, my wife and I ask our children (typically at dinner time) to share their most memorable experience from the vacation week. It's fun to not only recount our steps through so many fun activities, but the question also provides interesting insight into each of our children as individuals—inspirations, passions, new-found interests, and most importantly, which specific memories are burned in their minds and hearts.

What if we redefined part of our leadership approach and/or role in the workplace to be Chief Memory Maker? What if you "got under the hood" of the people you lead to really learn what memories were made in the work-place last week, or on your most recent project? Find out what memory is burned in their mind or heart, specifical-ly, from the work they did on that recent product launch.

Most people have an inherent desire to be part of a memory. Want proof? Open your video or photo files the week after vacation, and watch your entire family flock to your side for a sneak peek. The same dynamic exists in your office. You have the power to create the kind of memories that will last a lifetime.

What about your customers? Wouldn't it be interest-ing to ask them what they find most memorable about the last experience they had with your call center? Or what impressions they had the last time they visited your website or storefront?

Imagine where conversations such as these might take you and the people you lead. Two words: unchartered waters.

And that may be exactly the kind of leadership your organization and your family need right now.

Taking the Leap

Thankfully, three of my four children have grown to swim on their own now, without life jackets, arm floats, or needing to hang on to me so tightly that their finger-nails dig into my arm.

I remember the difficulty the kids had as they were learning to swim.

While I stood in the pool's waist-high water, they would tiptoe to the edge of the concrete and plead with me to move closer to them, almost as if when they finally did jump, they wanted me to catch them before they even hit the water. Their fear of what *might* happen after the leap kept them firmly planted on the patio, anxiously pacing back and forth.

> *At some point on your own journey, every meaningful growth initiative will require a leap of faith.*

Ultimately, my children put their trust and faith in me catching them. After they proved to themselves they could do it, their confidence grew, ultimately leading to a willingness to take more leaps.

When you step to the proverbial edge in your own life, how do you muster the confidence to make the jump? Who or what do you put your faith in, especially when you can't see the bottom?

> *The <u>act</u> of leaping is where the growth happens, not in the outcome of the leap.*

At some point on your own journey, every meaningful growth initiative will require a leap of faith—especially when it is something you have never done before.

While I am not suggesting carelessness in the assessment of risk with whatever your particular endeavor may be, I am suggesting that you reframe your view to focus on the *act* of leaping rather than what happens *after* the leap. The act of leaping is where the growth happens, not in the outcome of the leap. Aside from a simple lack of ambition, digging beneath the surface reveals two common fears that stifle the jump: the fear of the failed attempt, and the fear of what others will think.

So, how is it possible to give up your desire to control the outcome and focus exclusively on the leap?

First, recall from chapter 1 that growth is best envisioned as a *circle*, not as a straight line with a start and a finish line. All growth is iterative—meaning you start, you do, you learn, and you make adjustments—and you do it again. There is no finish line to sustainable growth. The one who works the circle of re-learning, re-invention, and re-commitment is the one who wins. Consistently.

> *All growth is iterative— meaning you start, you do, you learn, and you make adjustments—and you do it again.*

WORKBOOK

Chapter 4 Questions

Question: Who are the sparks in your organization? Who are the fire-builders in your organization? Which are you? Which do you want to be? Why?

_____

_____

_____

_____

_____

_____

_____

_____

_____

_____

_____

_____

Question: Do you display vulnerability to your team? Do you display vulnerability to your spouse and your children? If not, what is stopping you? In what ways does being vulnerable make you more approachable as a leader or team member?

_____

_____

_____

_____

_____

_____

_____

_____

_____

Question: What are one or two "valleys" you have walked through (personally or professionally)? How have these valleys impacted or shaped your leadership story?

_____

_____

_____

_____

_____

_____

_____

_____

_____

Question: Reflect on your answers to the last question. Given the valleys you have walked through, are you ready to share your leadership story? Who in your organization needs to hear your story? What about your family? Have they heard your story? If not, what are you waiting for?

_____

_____

_____

_____

_____

_____

_____

_____

_____

_____

_____

_____

_____

_____

_____

_____

_____

_____

_____

Question: Does your organization value coaching and ongoing development? If not, why not? How much time, weekly, do you spend coaching employees and team members? How much time do you spend, monthly, on talent assessment and development? What do your answers say about the results you and your organization may or may not be achieving?

_____

_____

_____

_____

_____

_____

_____

_____

_____

_____

_____

_____

_____

_____

_____

_____

_____

_____

Circle Back: Read *The Most Excellent Way to Lead* by Perry Noble! Don't get bogged down in safe ideas or what's fair; be servant-minded—yet bold—if you want to make a real difference. And make sure your organization has leaders who provide inspirational spark, as well as leaders who are effective fire-builders. Regardless of which kind of leader you are—or whether you're a bit of both—become intentional about connecting with the people at all levels within your organization. Challenge yourself to become more vulnerable, more open, and more approachable. Most importantly, share your leadership story!

Finally, remember good leaders build leaders. Make coaching, developing and growing people a priority. As you do that, view your growth and theirs as a *circle*, not as a straight line with a start and a finish. Remind yourself—and them—that all growth is iterative: you start, you do, you learn, and you make adjustments. And then you do it again. The leader who works the circle of re-learning, re-invention, and re-commitment is the one who wins. Always.

CHAPTER FIVE

Growing All-In:
Tips for Becoming a Growth-Driven Leader

Living in a "super-sizing" society can be exhausting. In the business world, leaders face constant pressure to "go big or go home." If an organization isn't trying to one-up the competition, it's trying to one-up its own previous performance.

But *thinking* big doesn't have to mean *going* big. Thus, in this chapter we look at tips for growing by "going small"—by thinking outside the box and recalibrating our focus.

Thinking Big, Shrinking to Grow

As a leader, it's your responsibility to challenge your team with never-ending, always-improving, "raise-the-bar" performance standards. Ask yourself: Do the people you lead think differently, bigger, bolder, and more often than they did when they began working for you?

Not only is this way of thinking an opportunity for you to differentiate yourself as a leader, but it's a way to drive growth, loyalty and trust in the people you lead— a rare feat in today's corporate America that is a musical chairs dance of performers

> *Sometimes we need to shrink in order to grow.*

focused on the next position, as opposed to a unified chase to fulfill potential.

Often, success in the workplace and "thinking bigger," in fact, mean "getting smaller." I realize this concept may seem counter-intuitive. However, when we take time to view things from a different vantage point, sometimes the unobvious doors, paths, or routes to new solutions reveal themselves. Sometimes we need to shrink to grow.

Thus, here are three not-so-common ideas to help your team "shrink" in order to grow. These ideas will take those you are leading out of the common, repetitive environment they are so used to, and will stretch everyone participating—and hopefully, ultimately, strengthen the team.

1. Take your team outdoors.

What was once a source of creative inspiration and fresh perspective has migrated indoors and glued itself to screens that inform, shape, influence and ultimately, confine us.

Make time to get outdoors for some fresh air. Arrange an afternoon for those under your leadership to experience something unusual—canoeing, paddle boarding, kayaking, or even hiking. Not only will you build a connection within the team, but being outdoors will also get you and your team away from the distraction and influence of mobile screens and devices, providing you an environment to think. Yes, to *think* as individuals, leaders, and teams.

2. Take your team to see a movie.

Skip Friday lunch and enjoy popcorn instead—take everyone on your team to see a comedy! Yes, I am serious! Not only will you enjoy getting out of the office, but you'll also laugh (if it's a good one) and form bonds with each other that will spill over in to the workplace.

The idea of shrinking or "becoming small" can open new perspective and vision for alternative or different ways to achieve a particular goal.

3. Take your team on a field trip.

Since when did we stop taking field trips? Elementary school? Bring the idea to the corporate environment. Find a non-competitive, non-overlapping industry or organization that might be faced with challenges similar to those you and your team are currently experiencing. Perhaps it is a manufacturing issue, a product development hurdle, or challenges in attracting the right talent—these are universal struggles for virtually any company in any industry. Partner your teams in a white board session to discuss and find solutions to the problems you're facing. You'll be amazed by the exchange, as well as the quality and freshness of ideas.

Each of these ideas seeks to remove the team from the suffocating pressure of the day-to-day environment in order to think. It's an amazingly simple strategy that can be used by anyone to think outside the box.

But be careful—you might just stretch the thinking and overall growth trajectory of the people you lead more then you anticipate!

As we'll explore further in the next section, this growth trajectory can encompass not only the mental and emotional but the physical self as well.

Can Exercise Make You a Better Leader?

When it comes to new ways of thinking, I'm continually impressed with the kinds of questions executives and business owners ask me in their efforts to grow and expand. Several months ago, an executive whom I greatly admire asked my opinion on the correlation between executives' physical health and the "health" of the organizations they lead.

You may be wondering: How does building your body connect with building organizations and people?

After cultivating a life-long passion and habit for a fitness regimen, as well as an always-on, "watch-what-you-eat" discipline, let me give you my personal opinion in one word:

Everything.

Exercise can make you a better leader.

Here's the deal: you can get the science-backed detail and the medical, psychological, and physiological case for exercise anywhere on the Internet. Launch a Google search asking, "Why should I exercise?" and be prepared for hours of reading.

Personal and professional growth is a significant precursor to organization growth. In other words, people growth drives business growth—not the reverse. Stated another way, the organization grows only if and when individuals grow.

> **People growth drives business growth— not the reverse.**

Similarly, personal growth has a ripple effect on the engagement, confidence and ambition employees bring to their work. Leadership is the spark to *all* of it. If it's not happening, recognized or talked about in your workplace, it's on you.

The key to driving individuals to take ownership of their personal development is encouraging them to exchange bad habits for good ones. Exercise is an easy win.

If you're driven to make a mark in leadership, then being fit will not only elevate your impact but also fundamentally change the trajectory of growth for you and the people you lead.

Exercise creates energy and stamina.

Though it might seem counter-intuitive, you must *use* energy to *gain* energy. This is why a person who sleeps a great deal often still complains of being tired.

After years of developing an afternoon exercise habit, I still find myself exercising at the end of the day. I can feel tired enough at the end of the day to go right to sleep; however, after exercising, I find it difficult to get to sleep.

Exercise creates energy. And energy makes a huge difference when you're leading people and families, doesn't it?

Exercise fuels focus.

In a world brimming with multiple distractions and demands at every turn, there are very few activities remaining that allow people to disconnect completely. Exercise removes your brain and your body from the desks, screens, calls, and endless multi-tasking. As a result, you will find your thoughts and focus during exercise move toward the most important priorities in your life. In essence, exercise sharpens your focus by helping you focus.

As I begin an exercise session, it's not uncommon for my mind to race, filled with lots of to-do's, tasks, and worries. But 30 to 45 minutes later, after exercising, most of those stressors and worries have whittled down to only those that truly matter. Following exercise, I have a clearer mind and am more focused.

Exercise drives confidence.

The most effective and influential leaders exude confidence. If you're not confident in yourself, it's impossible to express or have confidence in others.

Being physically fit builds self-confidence and self-esteem. Leaders with low self-esteem often lead from a defensive posture, failing to recognize others or address mistakes. Leaders with low self-esteem often use curt tones that discourage idea sharing in the workplace—unknowingly stifling the growth of others.

As exercise begins to change your body positively, it is reflected not only in the mirror, but also through compliments from others. And as you start to feel better about yourself, your confidence will increase at home and in the office—and thus, a different attitude will emerge. This changes everything.

Exercise unlocks influence.

Exercise releases key hormones in your brain that reduce stress and anxiety. Perhaps you've become accustomed to heavy bouts of daily stress that impact you personally, as well as the people around you. Unmanaged stress can have an adverse effect on you as a leader in terms of your relational skills with people, detracting from your influence. An exercise session, however, can quickly deflate heavy stress, leaving you calm, cool, and collected and allowing you to be at your influential best.

Exercise is contagious.

People admire those who have successfully transformed their physical and emotional shape, because they understand that such transformation requires fortitude, discipline, and perseverance. The achievement alone can inspire others, but more importantly, it establishes an example for personal growth that others will aspire to follow. As people around you begin to latch on to a movement for better health, the accountability to a "new normal" grows larger on the culture as a whole.

Exercise is a spark to creativity.

Most regular exercisers agree that some of their very best thoughts and ideas happen while exercising (which is certainly true for me as well). As mentioned above, exercise has an incredible releasing effect, helping individuals de-stress and prioritize life. This calming and clearing effect can open your mind and heart to possibilities and thoughts that spark creative ideas. Imagine an entire workforce engaged in this mode of thinking!

Exercise triggers the right habits.

When hard work pays off, it's rewarding. Exercise is no different. If you're looking for a starting point for big change, exercise is it. Building lean muscle mass and cardiovascular health is the sustainable path to long-term health. As you begin to feel physically and emotionally transformed, the positive results "hardwire" your brain and your body, and exercise becomes a habit.

Generally speaking, you want more of a good thing, right? Exercise is a precursor to other healthy habits—most commonly better nutrition and healthier eating habits. Subconsciously, the more you exercise and improve your health, the less you will want to do anything to damage the strong body you are building. Very rarely do you see a person leaving a gym lighting a cigarette. Could it be that a good habit can replace a bad habit?

It's not about you.

Your body was designed for activity. This is why it hurts, becomes sick, or is rendered immobile if you aren't active enough. You and I have been given only one body for the life and time we have on earth. You've also been called to be a leader over your organization and your family. There are people everywhere who need you to lead them. And that means you need to be here so you can lead them. So, in the end, fitness is not really about you.

And neither is leadership.

If you're already committed to being fit, you're certainly enjoying the benefits that I mentioned above. If you're not, what's keeping you from getting started? How valuable would it be to you to start a fitness program tomorrow?

Most importantly, what kind of leader might you become to the people in your life who matter most, at the office and at home?

You've been called. They need you to be 100 percent here. Now go be fit! You'll be glad you did. And so will they.

So, if exercise can make us better leaders, what about parenthood? Let's take a look.

Can Parenthood Make You a Better Leader?

I can guess what you're thinking right now: How in the world could building your family be connected with your ability to lead and build people in the workplace?

As a parent of four incredibly strong-willed, talented and (usually) loving children (ages eleven, nine, seven, and three), I'll cut right to the chase.

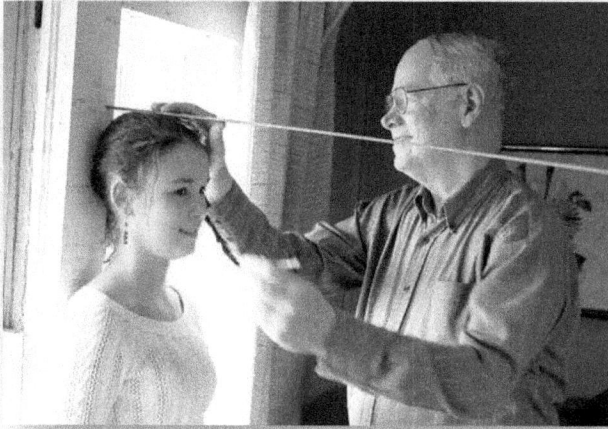

Parenthood builds a mindset for potential.

There's no better place to kick off the case for parenthood than the word *potential*. Every parent can relate to watching your children learn, experiment and play—wondering what they might one day become. As they grow, they become a bit

> *The best leadership helps others see their own potential.*

(or in both my sons' case, *a lot*) more daring, taking on monster jumps from countertops and tall tree forts—an "I can do anything and be anything I want" attitude. The mindset for potential is a beautiful thing ... while it lasts.

As we mature, however, negative outside influences seep through the cracks and eventually begin to infect and weaken this mindset for potential. This is the tall order for leaders. Whether leading a family or a workplace team, it's our calling and responsibility to eradicate the infections that attack potential. The best leadership helps others see their own potential.

Parenthood is a needed distraction.

While you may be nodding your head, it's not what you think. Removing the proverbial "office hat" and replacing it with the "parent hat" as you dive into parent-mode is a release and distraction from the daily grind at the office. For the moment, completely removing yourself from tie and coat to shoot basketball with your seven-year-old is liberating. You need a distraction from the challenges

> *Having patience to let potential develop and blossom at its own pace is the heart of leadership.*

you face on the battleground at the office, and for me, there's no better way than four children tugging at my pant leg to come play.

The way you know if your time with your children is quality time as opposed to multitasking is that you realize you've not thought about work for the first time all day. And that has a refueling effect on your leadership capacity for tomorrow, doesn't it?

Parenthood cultivates patience.

One of the most difficult aspects of leadership is patience. As a leader, you can see the top of the mountain and the path to arrive. The challenge, then, becomes not only taking your team up the mountain with you, but doing so at the same speed. If you have not yet experienced elementary school as a parent, be forewarned: it will require every bit of patience you can muster. These are the years when your children are learning to read, write, add and subtract, and they will do it with different learning styles, personalities and speed. Having patience to let potential develop and blossom *at its own pace* is the heart of leadership.

> *The very best leaders cultivate and encourage imagination.*

Parenthood cultivates imagination.

You know where I'm going with this one, don't you? If you're a parent, you've marveled at least once in the last week over something your child did that was off-the-charts imaginative. Imagine a nine-year-old who wants to play tackle football so badly that he inflates a pool float to use as a tackling dummy in the front yard. Yep, that kind of imagination happened at my house as neighbors drove by watching the whole thing.

At some point, as we become adults, we start worrying about what other people think. It's like a virus that completely wipes out our imagination and fearlessness to try new things. Shame on me—I'm surrounded by imagination at home and rarely recognize it, but I am frustrated to no end at the lack of it in the workplace. The very best leaders cultivate and encourage imagination.

Parenthood creates connection.

My assumption is that the large percentage of people who work for and with you are parents. An obvious way to connect with your people is to get to know them personally. Communicate with them. Tell them about your family and they will likely begin to tell you about their family, too.

> *The day you became a leader is when the spotlight sharply swung from you to the people you lead.*

Sharing parenting stories helps bring down walls and establishes common ground. Moreover, it demonstrates that you, as a leader, care about your team members' lives beyond the workplace. That's when leadership touches the sky.

Parenthood is a source of energy.

Hard to imagine, isn't it? Yes, parenting is draining (just ask my wife). And yes, time does often feel as if it's standing still in the day-to-day battles. It's when we take time to look back that we see nothing but change and growth. We see childhood stages evaporate and milestones shattered. Parenting is a source of energy because it's live growth in front of our eyes.

As leaders, we get revved up by the big growth story, don't we? But in order to see it, we need to stop, look back, and acknowledge how far we've come.

Parenthood is our purpose.

At the end of the day, leadership is about growth—in particular, the growth of people. The day you became a leader is when the spotlight sharply swung from you to the people you lead. You were charged—not with a responsibility—but with an *obligation* to grow others. It happened the day, hour and minute that your precious little daughter or son entered this world. Similarly, you were charged with the awesome responsibility to grow others the day you agreed to lead your team at work.

As a parent, it's been said that we put a lifetime of energy, time, and love into raising our children only to one day let them go. Sounds a lot like leadership.

Final Thoughts

However small it might be, my hope is that something here might be freeing enough for you to drop work at the door and sink everything you've got into building your family. As you stretch and develop your children to reach their potential, what you just might come to find is how close you are to realizing your own.

Plug into your children when you walk in the door after work tonight. Don't count the minutes you have until bedtime. Instead, get down on their level, in their space, and look into their eyes. And then try it again tomorrow and the next day. You'll be captivated and connected like never before.

And so will your people when you walk back into the office in the morning.

WORKBOOK

Chapter 5 Questions

Question: Do you agree or disagree: Does exercise make you a better leader? Why or why not? If you have a fitness routine, does it help you lead more effectively? If so, how? Do you need to make any adjustments in your exercise habits? If you don't exercise on a regular basis, what is getting in your way?

_____

_____

_____

_____

_____

_____

_____

_____

_____

_____

_____

Question: If you are a parent, list one or two ways parenting has made you, in your opinion, more effective as a leader. If you are not a parent, do you agree or disagree with the notion that parenting can make you a better leader? Why or why not?

_____

_____

_____

_____

_____

_____

_____

_____

_____

_____

_____

Circle Back: As a leader, you must make continuous, purposeful growth a constant priority. Think bigger by getting smaller. As we get smaller, we become more focused. Commit to building personal connections among your team members. Increase and expand your energy and confidence by implementing a simple fitness and exercise routine. Apply the lessons of parenthood to business leadership—focusing on patience, celebrating imagination, and developing personal potential.

CONCLUSION

A Different Kind of Hero

In this book, we've talked a lot about what drives growth. But, what drives *you*?

Over the last five chapters, we have focused on growth strategies and leadership content for business executives and corporate decision makers. However, it's worth taking a moment to highlight a different kind of lesson in growth. This kind of life-changing personal growth can only happen through deepening faith, continual prayer, and trust in God's remarkable plan for our lives.

As I write this, my wife, Lauri, and I recently celebrated our youngest daughter's third birthday. Her favorite six words are "I do it *all by myself*," followed closely by the phrase "Oh, that's delicious, mom!" (particularly in reference to anything with refined sugar as its main ingredient).

Lily's development has been especially precious to us, as she was welcomed into our family with great joy through the gift of adoption. 'Blessed' doesn't begin to scratch the surface in describing the way Lily has completed our family. And truly, her life gives new meaning to the words 'worth the wait.'

Nobody exhibited deeper faith or trust in God's path than Lily's moms—her birth mother, who was strong enough to let go, and Lauri, my wife and Lily's 'forever' mom, who was strong enough to catch. And God provided the strength in a big way. Both women represent an unconventional kind of hero—a hero driven to know God, to grow close to God and impact this world for God. Lauri is my hero—she not only showed me what deep faith looks like, but also re-defined for me the ultimate starting point for healthy growth: prayer.

For three years, Lauri prayed circles for our fourth child while fighting an uphill battle, dodging adoption obstacles fraught with pain and, truly, more twists and turns than a reality TV show. Yet she found a way to keep going even when it seemed as though all of the doors leading to adoption had been slammed closed. Like Peter stepping outside the boat, surrounded by crashing waves, Lauri kept her eyes on Jesus—and wow, did God ever deliver, despite the years of fear, disbelief, and seemingly unanswered prayers. Looking back now, we see so clearly: it took many "unanswered" prayers to lead us to the miracle of Lily. God was guiding us all along—not just to 'any' baby, but very deliberately to "our" Lily.

Holding a newborn whom you believe you will parent and then letting that baby go, returning home to an empty nursery, and telling your three waiting children they won't have a baby sister is perhaps one of the most painful memories we have shared as a family. But Romans 8:28 tells us: "And we know that in all things God works for the good of those who love him, who have been called according to his purpose" (NIV). Our adoption journey is certainly evidence of the truth of this verse—as well as of the wise counsel of Dick Peckham, an adoption attorney who helped us on our path to Lily and to whom we will forever be grateful. Thank you, Dick, for encouraging us to continue our faith journey!

Let me repeat: personal growth begets professional growth. Professional growth, in turn, leads to team growth and team growth drives company growth. If your personal growth is road-blocked, you can't possibly begin to think about expanding revenue.

I want to leave you with eight "drivers" for your high-performing growth engine. These are drivers that I believe elevate any person—wife, mother, husband, father, business executive, leader, or friend—from ordinary to hero:

Habits and Discipline

The act of choosing the right, repeatable habits in your daily routine is perhaps the single most vital ingredient in driving successful growth and transformation. If you wait until you *feel* like doing something, you likely will never do it. Habit and action-centered lives (and cultures) drive forward.

Purpose and Vision

Purpose and vision are the spark plug. If purpose is the *impact* your work has on your world, then vision is the *how* your world will look after impact. Purpose and vision give birth to meaning and passion. And people follow meaning and passion.

Leap of Faith

Do you have the kind of faith that can free you from paralyzing constraints, distractions, and fear? Any growth initiative worth chasing in your personal or professional life will, at some point, require a leap of faith. When the clouds haven't parted and the fog hasn't lifted, will your faith carry you?

Honesty

Can you hold the person in the mirror accountable for what you said you would do, for the goals and plans you laid that had no action, for the people who entrusted you with their lives, and for who you are today and who you say you will be tomorrow?

Encouragement

Do you build others up? Do you have someone who builds you up? Quite simply, people go a lot further when someone else thinks they can.

Unquenchable Curiosity

Are you willing to learn, unlearn and relearn? Big ideas are very often inspired by and through sources outside your organization or immediate lives. Curious people stay in a permanent zone of discomfort—they live with a flexible comfort zone that easily stretches and expands. In turn, so does everything else.

Focus

An old Chinese proverb nails it: "Try to chase two rabbits at the same time and they both get away." Deep and narrow, or wide and shallow?

Prayer

If purpose and vision are the spark plug, then prayer is the fuel source for the engine. We have the incredible opportunity to take our biggest dreams and greatest fears to our heavenly Father for wisdom, guidance, and strength. Courage is fear saying a prayer. Are you praying circles around your life? Your business? Are others praying for you?

These eight "drivers" are mission-critical to you, your professional development, and your team. Without them—and God's grace—my wife Lauri and I would never have known the precious blessing of our daughter Lily.

Are you willing to be a hero, too? Just an ordinary person who is willing to do ordinary things in an extraordinary way—things that are sometimes hard, yet are vital for growth? And will you consider following Jesus into the darkest night and the deepest valley, where no one else has the answers—trusting Him and His truth to lead you?

Remember that growth begins, in part, with the paramount, fundamental truth of honesty—*who you are* and *how you live your life*. This is what drives everything, not only in the workplace but also in life—including your marriage, your parenting, your friendships, and your relationship with your Maker.

Without honesty in how you approach your personal identity and your personal life, growth will be stifled. With it, the potential for sustainable growth is limitless! You might even find yourself growing into the role of a hero for someone close to you, as my wife did for me.

So, what are you waiting for? Let's grow for it!

REFERENCES

Notes

1. Occelli, Cynthia. *Resurrecting Venus*. Goodreads. https://www.goodreads.com/author/quotes/5812884.Cynthia_Occelli
2. Dunne, Carey. "What Are Americans Most Stressed Out About?" *Fast Company*. 14 July 2014. http://www.fastcodesign.com/3032931/infographic-of-the-day/what-are-americans-most-stressed-out-about
3. Kegan, Robert, Lisa Lahey, Andy Fleming, and Matthew Miller. "Making Business Personal." *Harvard Business Review*. April 2014. https://hbr.org/2014/04/making-business-personal
4. McGrath, Rita. "This Year's Top Three Strategic Challenges." Interview video clip. In Todd Garretson, "This Year's Top Three Strategic Challenges," *CircleMakers.com*, 12 March 2014. http://circlemakers.co/this-years-top-three-strategic-challenges-video/

5. Williams, Robin. In "Robin Williams Quotes." *BrainyQuote.* http://www.brainyquote.com/quotes/quotes/r/robinwilli383827.html

6. Maslow, Abraham. In "Abraham Maslow > Quotes > Quotable Quotes." *Goodreads.* Goodreads, Inc. http://www.goodreads.com/quotes/7660537-in-any-given-moment-we-have-two-options-to-step

7. Montini, Laura. "The Innovation Strategies That Lead to Success." *Inc.* Inc.com. http://www.inc.com/laura-montini/infographic/what-really-fosters-innovation.html. Originally in "Infographic: What Really Fosters Innovation," *Column Five.* http://www.columnfivemedia.com/work-items/infographic-what-really-fosters-innovation

8. The Disney Institute and Theodore Kinni. *Be Our Guest*, 2011. In George Ciotti, "How Disney Creates Magical Experiences (and a 70% Return Rate)." *Huffington Post*, 21 April 2015. http://www.huffingtonpost.com/gregory-ciotti/how-disney-creates-magica_b_7093682.html

9. Buss, Dale. "'Chief Growth Officer' Title Catches On as a Way to Battle Growth Challenges." *Chief Executive.* ChiefExecutive.net. 15 August 2014. http://chiefexecutive.net/chief-growth-officer-title-catches-way-battle-growth-challenges/

10. Birol, Andy. "How to Know a Business Owner Is about to Fall from Grace (and What to Do about

It)." *Upstart Business Journal.* 4 March 2014. http://www.bizjournals.com/bizjournals/how-to/growth-strategies/2014/03/business-owner-falls-from-grace.html

11. Brandon, John. "20 Quotes on How Your Business Must Change by 2020." *Inc.* Inc.com. 21 April 2015. http://www.inc.com/john-brandon/20-quotes-on-how-your-business-must-change-by-2020.html

12. "Executive." *Dictionary.com.* http://www.dictionary.com/browse/executive?s=. Originally from *Online Etymology Dictionary*, Douglas Harper, 2010.

13. "Process." *Dictionary.com.* http://www.dictionary.com/browse/process?s=t

14. Kaplan, Robert S., and Norton, David P. *Creating the Office of Strategy Management.* Working paper. Harvard Business School, July/August 2005. http://www.hbs.edu/faculty/Publication%20Files/05-071.pdf

15. Mankins, Michael, and Richard Steele. "Turning Great Strategy into Great Performance." *Harvard Business Review*, 2005. Cited in Dewey, Barbara (ed.), *Transforming Research Libraries for the Global Knowledge Society*, Elsevier, 2010, p. 72.

16. Noble, Perry. *The Most Excellent Way to Lead.* Tyndale, 2016.

17. Cook, Jeffrey. "Delta and America Airlines Banning Hoverboards." *ABCNews.* 10 December 2015. http://abcnews.go.com/US/delta-air-lines-banned-hoverboards/story?id=35699893

18. Korb, Alex. In Malloy, Mark, "5 Simple Habits That Will Make You Feel Better." *The Telegraph*. Telegraph Media Group Limited. http://www.telegraph.co.uk/news/science/120547 44/The-five-secrets-to-happiness-according-to-science.html

19. Brown, Brené. "The Power of Vulnerability." TEDxHouston. *TED*. TED Conferences, LLC. June 2010. http://www.ted.com/talks/brene_brown_on_vulnerability

20. Brown, Brené. *Ibid.*

21. Stanley, Andy. "Ask It: Time over Time." *North Point Community Church*. North Point Ministries, Inc. 19 Jan. 2014. http://northpoint.org/messages/ask-it/time-over-time

22. Bersin, Josh. "Spending on Corporate Training Soars: Employee Capabilities Now a Priority." *Forbes*. Forbes Media LLC. 4 February 2014. https://www.forbes.com/sites/joshbersin/2014/02/04/the-recovery-arrives-corporate-training-spend-skyrockets/#c5a736dc5a73

About the Author

Todd Garretson, founder and Chief Growth Strategist of CircleMakers, has a passion for unlocking dormant growth potential in individuals, teams, and organizations. A growth strategist by nature, Todd specializes in building high-performance organizations as well as helping owners and executives with strategic growth development.

You can find Todd at the intersection of the architect and the builder—with the unique ability both to envision growth and to make it come to life. As a Strategic Advisor, Todd maps a strategy and then guides leaders and their organizations to break through growth plateaus, challenges, and barriers en route to realizing their full potential—and, ultimately, increased financial and marketplace results.

Todd spent the first decade of his career building, expanding, and eventually selling a family manufacturing business. He went on to serve in a number of corporate management roles, leading strategy, marketing, and growth initiatives for Hunter Douglas and Newell Rubbermaid.

Having been immersed in a mid-size family manufacturing business alongside his father and brother since childhood, and having then transitioned to corporate America and back again to business owner, Todd understands the challenges involved in managing and growing large and small businesses alike. He also understands the complex role of the leadership team in the organization.

Todd brings a deep knowledge base and extensive expertise in navigating business owners and executive teams through unique growth challenges to achieve record-setting organizational results. Moreover, he brings a heart for his clients and their customers. Todd believes, ultimately, organizations don't change until the people in them change.

Residing in Atlanta, Georgia, with his wife, Lauri, and their four children, Todd spends his weekends and free time with family, coaching youth sports, and sharing his passion for fitness, nutrition, and faith.

Todd is available for guest writing, speaking engagements with audiences of all sizes, and various board and advisory assignments.

To learn more about Todd, visit www.toddgarretson.com.

About CircleMakers

At the heart of every great growth story is a big, bold dream with lots of circles around it.

For a variety of reasons, unmet potential is commonplace in businesses everywhere. Whether it be obstacles, artificial limitations, distractions, or fear, we let the small swallow the big.

Close to 90% of organizations fail to ever realize the full value of their strategies. The widest gap in business today is that between strategy and results.

Does your organization have a growth strategy? One of the biggest misconceptions is that your strategic plan is your strategy—but this couldn't be further from the truth!

Does running your business get in the way of building your business?

Do you find your business delivering inconsistently on top- and bottom-line performance, year in and year out?

Are you susceptible to flavor-of-the-month management and multiple changes in direction?

Do you find your business spends too much time on what the competition is doing and not enough time on your customers' needs?

Are you getting innovative ideas from all levels of the organization on how to serve your customers more effectively?

How will you bring your organization's vision to life?

Will you be able to mobilize your team in a specific direction, behind the right activities, in order to deliver the results you envision?

Very few organizations can claim success in any of these areas.

The good news? There's a way forward *that works*. It's time to move from inspiration to reality.

CircleMakers is a strategy advisory firm that helps organizations drive stronger performance and growth.

Through a portfolio of custom advisory services, we bring deep expertise that enables organizations to identify new growth potential, craft strategy that moves people to action, and enhance overall performance.

We've helped organizations mobilize and elevate their brands in multi-billion dollar markets, establishing a path to consistent double-digit revenue growth.

We work across a wide array of industries, including retail, hospitality, consumer products, manufacturing, construction, building products, non-profits, and service organizations. Our expertise ranges from family-owned businesses to private equity portfolio companies to publicly-held businesses, and our experience encompasses organizations anywhere from $1 million to over $1 billion in size.

In addition to our custom strategy consulting, Circle-Makers.co is an online destination and multi-media strategy resource for growth-oriented executives, business owners, CEOs, and professionals. Our mission is to equip owners with tools, inspiration, best practices, and practical resources that can be accessed and applied against their business challenges.

For more information, visit us: www.circlemakers.co.

About Speak It To Book

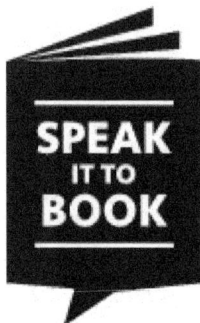

Speak It to Book is revolutionizing how books are created and used.

Traditional publishing requires thousands of hours, and then you're asked to surrender your rights. Self-publishing is indicative of a poor-quality product with no prestige. And neither model boasts results-driven marketing.

That's why we created a better option. Speak It To Book has the attention of the industry because we are disrupting it in a brilliant way.

Your ideas are meant for a wider audience. So step into significance—by speaking your story into a book.

Visit www.speakittobook.com to learn more.

www.ingramcontent.com/pod-product-compliance
Lightning Source LLC
LaVergne TN
LVHW051549080426
835510LV00020B/2924